IT'S A
TEEN'S LIFE

Money and Life Skills That Every American Teenager Needs to Know

Mark Delahunty

It's a Teen's Life: Money and Life Skills That Every American Teenager Needs to Know.
Copyright © 2016 by Mark Delahunty.

ISBN-10:0-9978055-0-1

ISBN-13:978-0-9978055-0-5

Healthcare Business Institute Publishing Company

9350 SW 137th Avenue, Suite 513

Miami, FL 33186.

(888) 423-6542

*All proceeds generated from the sales of this book
will be used towards creating additional awareness in
high schools throughout the United States*

DISCLAIMER

This publication is designed to provide accurate and author-itative information in regard to the subject matter covered. It is sold with the understanding that the publisher is not engaged in rendering legal, accounting, or other profes-sional service. If legal advice or other expert assistance is required, the services of a competent professional person should be sought.

Links in this book are provided as a convenience and for informational purposes only. All links are current at the time of publication. Author makes no guarantee links will work at a later date.

ACKNOWLEDGMENTS

As always, I remain grateful to my three children, Kayla, Logan, and Alexa Delahunty, for the inspiration they provide me every day, simply by being who they are. I want to dedicate this book to my children, and also to Miranda and Gabriella Carreras; Bianca and Carolina Lopez-Lima, as the daughters of my true love, my soulmate, and my best friend, Marta Lopez. Without her influence and encouragement, this book would not have been published, would not be available to benefit millions of teenagers who will read it, and as a result, will make better personal financial decisions.

I would also like to acknowledge my parents, Christine and Raymond Delahunty, as well as my "second parents," Cynthia and Alan Williams, for always supporting me, believing in me, and loving me the way they do.

CONTENTS

ABOUT THE AUTHOR

Mark Delahunty was born and raised in the United Kingdom. He was an avid rugby player and an international chess player at a very young age.

On October 18, 1992, in Wales, United Kingdom, Mark was involved in a major car accident. He was only eighteen years old. He suffered with collapsed lungs and received numerous heart resuscitations. He lapsed into a coma which lasted for three long weeks. Once he came out of the coma, what followed was two weeks of intense rehabilitation.

Sometime after the accident, Mark was offered an opportunity to move to the United States. He was then educated at the University of Wisconsin-Parkside, earning his Bachelor's degree in Sociology. He went on to attend Florida Atlantic University where he studied at the Master's level, earning a degree in Public Administration. At present, Mark is studying for his terminal-degree level of education, a Doctorate of Health Administration at Central Michigan University.

Mark has worked more than twenty years in healthcare, specializing in hospitals, dialysis outpatient treatment centers, and laboratories. He has traveled around the world, gaining an understanding of the healthcare systems in Europe, North America, South America, Australia, and Asia.

He has owned and sold his own businesses, worked as a

University Professor at an international university, and now has retired from the traditional corporate business world to pursue his own new business ventures – ventures that contribute to society. One of those ventures is to become an author who helps to influence the success of others. This is Mark's first book.

PREFACE

I have written this book to address a significant need throughout the United States of America and around the world. I find that students are not being taught in school the basic money and life skills needed to make good financial decisions. Instead, our young adults are having to learn through the rugged "school of hard knocks." This being the case, they end up making costly mistakes that can result in life-long debt. Some even wind up having their possessions, such as cars, homes, and furniture, taken from them. Some file bankruptcy, and many go into their later years with no money saved for retirement.

My take on this? It doesn't have to be this way.

For the basis of this book, I draw upon my own expertise and my experiences as a healthcare chief executive officer, a business entrepreneur, and university professor (having studied at the doctorate level).

My goal is to provide a simple understanding of everyday areas of personal finance that will be educational, inspirational, and motivational, to help teens make better decisions–decisions that could bring about a successful financial future.

The book also provides a touch of reality about teens

being true to themselves to live within their means, and to be willing to make necessary sacrifices that will benefit them later in life.

Examples provided throughout the book are ones that have worked for me using sources of information in which I have knowledge. I make no claim that these are the only options, or even the best options available. What I am saying is that this knowledge has served me well and can work for you. This information can be used as a great foundation to compare new tools, reports, technology, and resources that might become available after the publication of this book.

The relevance of this book may not apply to residents of other countries. It is best suited for natural-born citizens of the United States of America. In full disclosure, much of the content of this book is a compilation of work from other authors that I researched on relevant topics, and felt they provided great information to enhance the learning experience of the reader. I do not intend for this book to be perceived as solely my own work; therefore, references are provided in each chapter.

I am aware there are other financial books out there that target teenagers, and there are authors who have published on each topic discussed in this book. However, to my knowledge, this is the only book for teens that covers all the chapter topics that are included here.

Travis, the character created for this book, is heading into his senior year of high school, and experiences many of the same struggles, confusion, challenges, and choices that you face in your life. Travis is joined by his cousin, Joey, who is six-months younger. (Six months can seem like a lifetime when you're waiting to get your driver's license!)

Travis's younger sister, Allie, makes an appearance here and there in the book, as does Joey's older brother, Craig, who is home from college for the summer. Now that Craig has two years of college under his belt, he sees himself as worldly wise–but Joey only sees him as a know-it-all. (If you have older siblings, you get the drift here.)

As an added note, all the proceeds from the sale of this book will be used towards creating financial and life skills awareness at high schools throughout the United States.

INTRODUCTION

Each chapter within this book can stand alone to help educate teens throughout their life to make more informed and responsible financial decisions. However, the book is also designed as a roadmap to touch on key financial and life skill decisions every individual will face on their life's journey, and provide helpful information and solutions for each stage encountered.

As you grow up, you will need different forms of identification for people to confirm who you are, for example when you get a job, or buy a car or home. You will need to find a job to make money to meet your financial obligations, and then need a strategy to manage your money.

There are many financial mistakes to avoid throughout your life, and you will need to make major investments and sacrifices to prepare for your future in the event you become too old to work, or are prohibited from work due to poor health conditions.

Life is tough, but the information in this book gives you an advantage to become financially secure for the rest of your life, protect your wealth, and understand the important financial decisions you will have to make.

CHAPTER 1

MAY I SEE YOUR ID?

Travis reached for his iPhone to turn down the volume on the music. Propped up in his bed, he was reading a fascinating WWII novel, and the music was spoiling his concentration. At that moment, the door of his bedroom flung open and his cousin, Joey, burst into the room.

"Hey Trav! What's going on? Reading? You're reading!" Joey slapped his forehead and rolled his eyes in typical Joey-drama fashion. "It's summer vacation, for Pete's sake. What are you, nuts or something?"

Travis looked up. He was used to his cousin's interruptions–the two were more like brothers than cousins. They lived only a few blocks apart, and were usually both at one house or the other.

"Thanks for knocking."

Joey plopped down on the foot of the bed. "Knocking's for guests. Back to my question. Are you nuts? Reading when you should be enjoying summer?"

"I enjoy reading. And I love history."

"Argh."

Travis, knowing his quiet moment was now ended, laid the book down. "To what do I owe the pleasure of this rude interruption?"

"Good news!" Joey pulled his wallet from his back pocket. "Your lucky day. I'm paying back the twenty I borrowed last week."

"It wasn't last week. It was two weeks ago. And you just as well keep it. You'll be borrowing it again in a few days."

"Hey, that's not nice. Here." He thrust the bill at Travis. "You tuck it under the flap in your wallet. For later. Just in case."

Grabbing the twenty, Travis gave a snort. It was always this way. No matter how much money Joey earned, or received as an allowance, he was always short on cash.

Just then, something in Joey's wallet caught Travis's attention. "Let me see your wallet a minute."

"No sense looking. It's empty. I promise."

"Something else. Let's see."

Joey handed over this wallet. Travis pulled out Joey's Social Security card. "What's this doing in your wallet?"

"Silly question. I'm carrying it in my wallet. What's the big deal?"

"Craig told me..."

"Oh Craig. What does he know? Just because he's had a couple years of college you'd think he's earned his PhD."

Travis leaned over and gave Joey a shove, nearly knocking him off the bed. "If you listen, I'll tell you. Your older brother is a lot smarter than you give him credit for."

"All right. All right. Lay it on me, I'm all ears."

"The big deal is that if your wallet gets into the wrong hands, you can change credit card numbers, or bank information, but it's impossible to change your Social Security number. That number is called a *unique identifier.* That means the number is unique to you, and only you. With your Social Security number and little else, a smart thief can steal your identity, open new accounts in your name, work under your name, create new driver's licenses or state IDs in other states…"

"Okay, okay. I get it. Sheesh." Taking back his wallet, Joey added, "But that is sorta scary, isn't it?"

"Well, yeah. Your identity is important and needs to be protected." Travis picked his book back up. "This time Craig was right."

"One time. But please don't tell him I said so. Don't want to inflate his ego any more than it already is. He may explode." Joey headed for the door. "C'mon. Let's go do something fun!"

Travis tucked in a bookmark and laid the book aside. Arguing with Joey was an exercise in futility.

· · · · · ● · · · · ·

The Need for Proof of Identity

The exchange between Travis and his cousin may have saved Joey a lot of grief down the road. Your identification is extremely important–especially in this day and time, and in our culture.

You may know who you are, but others do not; and unfortunately there are many people in the world who pretend to be someone they are not. They steal an identity from someone else in order to commit financial crimes and fraud which can eventually land them in prison.

You will always need to prove who you are; therefore, this chapter focuses on the main documents accepted to prove your identity and guidance as to how to obtain each of them.

There are membership cards, bank cards, employee ID cards, student ID cards, and many other cards with your information and photograph that you will be required to obtain throughout your life. I won't cover all of those, but will focus our discussion on the documents that are the most important. As Travis pointed out–and as Joey learned–it's important to keep all your documents protected and safe at all times.

Even if you are in your teen years, it's never too early to take on this responsibility, and to take it seriously.

Five Common Forms of Identity

There are five common forms of identification that you will need throughout your life as a natural-born citizen of the United States:

1. Birth Certificate
2. Passport
3. Social Security Card
4. State Identification Card
5. State Driver's License

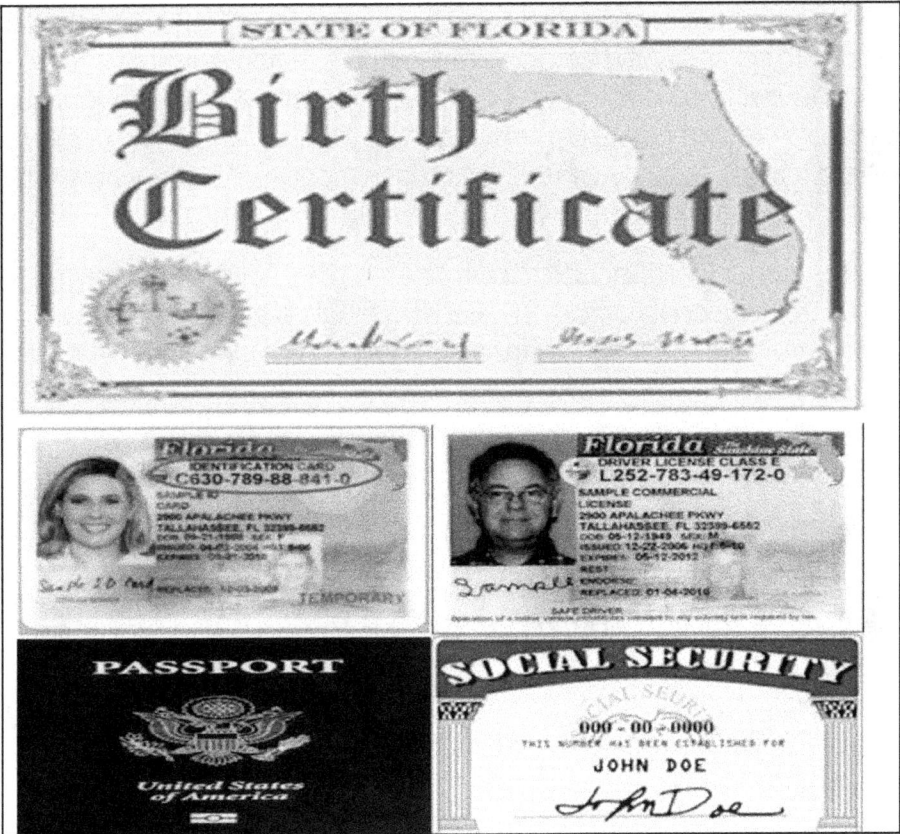

Each State is Similar–But Different

Each state has its own website for obtaining the different forms of identification; however, the process and requirements are similar in each state. Since I live in Florida, I have included websites that pertain to that state to obtain the information for you in this chapter. Since each state does have different requirements, simply do a Google search for your state. For example, search for *California and Driver's License* to come up with the requirements of that state and to get the documents you need.

Birth Certificate

Your birth certificate is the most important document you'll need to prove your legal identity and age. You'll need it to apply for a passport or government benefits, enroll in school, join the military, or claim pension or insurance benefits. If your parents do not have an original copy (ask them first), you will need to get a copy of your birth certificate. Where you were born will determine how to get it.

To get a certified copy of your birth certificate, contact the *vital records office* in the state where you were born. There you will receive instructions on how to request a copy and information on any fees. Go to the *National Center for Health Statistics* website for information on obtaining a birth certificate in your state:

www.cdc.gov/nchs/w2w/index.htm.

At the website, choose your state from the list and click on it. It will tell you how much it costs to request a birth certificate ($9 in Florida), the mailing address to send letters and applications, and what forms of identification you need to include. They also provide a phone number to call if you have questions.

Passport

A passport is an internationally recognized travel document that verifies your identity and nationality. A valid U.S. passport is required to enter and leave most foreign countries, as well as to return to the United States. Only the U.S. Department of State has the authority to grant, issue, or verify, U.S. passports.

> *NOTE: You only have one life to live. My strong recommendation is that you enjoy it and that you see as much of the world as possible to learn about other cultures and people.*

For information on applying for a US passport and

downloading (or submitting online) the required DS-11 Application for a U.S. Passport, go to the following website:

https://travel.state.gov/content/passports/en/passports/apply.html

You can also obtain an application from your local US post office or often at the local library. The cost for a passport book is $110, plus a $25 execution fee. There is no additional charge to have it sent to your home as standard delivery mail.

In addition to the application form, you must submit an original certified U.S. Birth Certificate. You also need a passport photograph (not just any snapshot). You can have a passport photo taken at a local CVS or Walgreens. The photograph must meet the exact requirements for color, size, photo-quality paper, portrait, acceptable clothing attire, etc. No selfies will meet the requirements, but fortunately stores that advertise passport photographs are aware of these requirements and will be able to help you.

The website will also allow you to search for a local Passport Acceptance facility by entering your zip code: https://travel.state.gov/content/passports/en/passports/apply.html.

The next step is to gather your completed application form, application fee, certified supporting documents and photograph, and submit your application. It usually takes about six weeks for the passport to be processed and sent to you. This means you will need to plan any out-of-the-US vacations well in advance.

You may also contact the *National Passport Information Center* (NPIC) for any other questions at 1-877-487-2778 or by email: NPIC@state.gov.

Social Security Card

As Travis explained to Joey, a Social Security number is a unique nine-digit number assigned to you and no one else.

It's important because you will need it to get a job, collect Social Security benefits, and receive other government services. Many businesses such as banks and credit companies ask for your number.

To apply for a Social Security card, complete an Application for a Social Security Card (Form SS-5) which you can download from the internet. Take or mail the completed application to your local Social Security office, along with two certified original documents by the issuing agency showing you are a United States Citizen (such as your birth certificate and passport). There is no charge for a Social Security number and card.

You should always treat your Social Security number as confidential information and avoid giving it out unnecessarily. Keep this card in a safe place with your other important papers. Don't carry it with you unless you need to show it to an employer or service provider.

To contact Social Secuirty for more information, or details when you're ready to obtain a number and card (such as downloading the form or locating a local office), go to their website: https://www.ssa.gov/. You can also call them at 1-800-325-0778 between the hours of 7am and 7pm Monday through Friday.

State Identification Card

A state identification is not quite as well-known as, say, your driver's license. But they are easy to acquire and can be a great source of identification—especially if, for some reason, you don't have a driver's license.

In Florida, ID cards are issued by the Department of Highway Safety and Motor Vehicles (DHSMV). You can check in your state to know which agency issues state identification cards. The information below will be similar for your state. Just Google your state name and state ID card to obtain the agency name and website.

A State ID card proves your age, identity, or residence, for many everyday activities such as making purchases on a credit card, boarding commercial airplanes, signing contracts, and banking. State ID cards can also be very helpful during emergencies–such as automobile accidents or cases of missing persons–and qualify as a federal form of identification.

Once a person has a valid state driver's license, having a state ID card is no longer necessary and it needs to be cancelled. In some states, people as young as five years old can obtain a state ID card.

To obtain a Florida State ID card, schedule an appointment online at your local office by going to:

https://services.flhsmv.gov/Oasis/

You will need to bring proof of your identity such as a valid, unexpired U.S. Passport or Certified Birth Certificate, your Social Security Card, and proof that you live in Florida such as a lease/rent agreement or utility bill. The cost is $25 for a new card, plus $6.25 office fee.

Driver's License

There's hardly a teenager alive that doesn't count the days (sometimes the hours, as well) until they are able to take the wheel with license in hand and have the freedom to come and go as they please. (Well, at least within the family rules).

Every state has a *Department of Motor Vehicles Department* (or the equivalent), and will have a website where you can find out all the answers about getting your driver's license. The best source for information for those living in Florida is: http://www.dmv.org/fl-florida/teen-drivers.php.

Requirements will vary some from state to state, but for the purposes of an example, as I previously stated, I'll use

Florida regulations here. The law in Florida states that first-time drivers must take a Florida driver's education course prior to applying for a license there. This site is a good choice for Florida driver education: http://www.floridadrivingcourse.com/.

You can enroll in this four-hour class from home and complete it at your convenience. This course teaches how alcohol and other drugs affect your ability to drive, Florida laws and responsibilities, safe driving techniques, and how to increase your awareness on Florida's roadways.

After completing the online course, you'll be prepared to take the written exam online at your local Florida DMV office. To find your nearest office, go to: http://www.florida-drivingcourse.com/ and enter your home zip code.

NOTE: Please see the Appendix for the list of restrictions that Florida requires.

Other States

I have used my home state of Florida as an example here, but keep in mind that every state is different. Check with the DMV in your state for the rules and restrictions that will apply to you.

Congratulations!

Once you have obtained all these forms of identification, then congratulations are in order—a huge milestone has been reached to prepare you for the rest of your life. You will just need to renew your driver's license from time to time based on the expiration date.

Now that you understand about identification, what it is, and why it's necessary, let's look at how you might find a job and start earning your own money.

CHAPTER 2

IT'S ALL ABOUT EARNING
THE MONEY

Travis's fingers were fairly flying over the keys of his laptop. He and Joey were sitting at a corner booth of their favorite coffee shop where Wi-Fi was available. Joey was working intently with his iPad. Neither noticed as Craig came in the shop, placed his order for black coffee, and walked over to their booth.

"I could feel the brain vibes the second I walked in the door. What's going on here?"

Travis looked up. "Hey Craig. We're in money-making mode. Gotta find summer jobs."

Craig shook his head. "Would have been smarter if you'd started looking a month or so ago."

Joey barely glanced up at his older brother. "We can't always be as perfect as you, Craig."

"Craig's right, you know," Travis said. "But, listen Craig, that last semester of school was rugged. All I was thinking about was grades."

Since neither boy offered to scoot over and make room in the booth, Craig pulled up a chair and sat down. "So what are you looking for in the way of jobs?"

"I'm applying at Lester's Foods as a stocker."

"And what made you choose Lester's?" Craig wanted to know.

"Locally owned—not a big franchise. They're always friendly and the employees seem to enjoy working there."

"Good reasons, Trav. I can see you starting as a stocker and moving up to cashier in no time." Craig took a sip of his coffee. "And what about you, Joey? Where are you applying? Or are you looking for the newest movie releases?"

Travis stopped what he was doing and looked over at Joey's iPad. "I wouldn't doubt it—movie buff that he is."

Joey picked up the iPad to move it out of view. "You two stop teaming up against me. For your information, I *am* looking for ways to make money, but none of that hourly-wage, answer-to-a-boss stuff for me. I'm more the entrepreneurial type, so I'm looking for ways to make money online. You can't imagine how many opportunities there are to make money on the net."

Craig shook his head. "Yeah. And you can't imagine how many are nothing but scams."

Joey looked over at Travis. "What'd I tell you? Always comes on with the negative." To Craig, he said, "For your information, I learned about these money-makers from a guy in my chemistry class. A guy I happen to trust."

"Is he making any money?"

"Well, not yet. These things take time."

Craig stood up and returned the chair to the other table. "I hate to leave this happy party but I have to get to work myself."

"Hey man," Travis said, "I may need a little help getting this application filled out right. Could you...?"

"Sure. No problem. Want me to stop over after I get off work this evening?"

"That'd be great. I really want this job."

"No problem. And Joey?"

"Yes, all-wise big brother?"

"There really are a lot of scams out there. You may be the entrepreneurial type, but the best idea is to get a regular job, get some cash coming in, then use that cash to research business opportunities." He turned to go, then added. "Just promise me you won't spend money you don't have."

"Sure, sure, bro. Whatever you say."

· · · · ● ● ● · · ·

The Job Search

It happens to all teens—some younger, some older—but sooner or later they start looking for ways to earn their own spending money. Some start out mowing lawns, babysitting, or doing odd jobs. Some learn how to handle money because they've received an allowance.

In this chapter we'll talk about the job search and give a few interviewing tips. Of course life is not all about money, but it is certainly needed to live life. The greater your income, the more choices life affords you and the more opportunities you can create for yourself.

I encourage you to always strive for the highest-paying position you can obtain, to create the most income possible for yourself, while at the same time being true to your own ability, aspiration level, and job satisfaction. Life is too short to get stuck in a job that you hate, which in turn makes you dread getting up each morning. Below is a great formula for you to remember:

Satisfaction in what you do +
maximum income potential realized =
the winning formula

Resume

You may be in the same place as Travis and Joey—you're ready to launch out and get that job. But wait. First you will need a resume. Well, at least you should get familiar with what a resume is and how to create one.

A resume is a document that summarizes your experience, skills, education, and other information. The purpose of a resume is to demonstrate that you are a perfect candidate for a position you are applying for. For most teens, the resume may be relatively brief as you've not had time in your life to have much job experience. However, you can definitely include your personality strengths, your talents and skills, and any extracurricular activities you're involved in. These all point to the fact that you're a well-rounded individual.

Your resume is written by you, not by someone else. It should be formal, professional, and relevant. For examples and tips for on how to write your first resume, check out this website:

www.hloom.com/download-free-sample-template-high-school-resume

Ideas and Suggestions for Finding a Job

In this section, I've included a few of my ideas and recommendations regarding finding a job:

- Make a list of things you love to do. What comes naturally for you? What might others pay you to do? Keep this list handy so you can refer back to it.

- Let your family members, friends and other acquaintances know that you're looking for a job, and ask if they know of any open positions. Your personal network is always the best first step. This is a good lesson early on about how important it is to have good relations with people you meet. Be kind and courteous to people you meet, and continue to make friends and build relationships throughout your professional career. (This is known in the business world as *networking*.) Keep a file of contact information for your network so you can call on them at any time as necessary in the future.

- Look in your local newspaper job-posting section in the classified ads

- Think about the things you like to do and the interests you have (refer to your list mentioned above). Visit those types of businesses—walk in and introduce yourself. Ask to talk to a manager or someone in the human resources department. Check to see if they have any open positions. Dress appropriately and bring along a copy of your resume.

- In this day and age of technology, it's easy to apply for jobs online. Seek out the company or industry in which you're interested. Apply on their website for open positions listed in your area. Complete applications in great detail. The information they see says a lot about your efforts.

- Look for help-wanted signs on storefronts

- Post your resume on career websites and search available openings in your area to apply (www.LinkedIn.com, www.Careerbuilder.com, www.Monster.com, https://www.theladders.com/)

- Consider starting your own business. Determine a service need in your community and start marketing yourself to build a customer base. For instance:

  ○ Walking dogs

  ○ Mowing lawns

  ○ Washing windows

  ○ Garage cleaning

  ○ House sitting (people go on vacation in summer and hate to leave their house empty)

  ○ Babysitting

  ○ Teaching younger kids what you're good at: music lessons, remedial math, computer skills, etc.

  ○ Helping at a day care

  ○ Serving the elderly

  ○ And so on... you get the idea

It's important to get your foot on the career ladder and start to gain experience to add to your resume. Pursue new opportunities as they present themselves and for which you feel you are ready.

Keep in mind, as I mentioned at the outset, these are ideas and suggestions that can be used to find your job. No matter how you find that first job, always be thankful that you are not one of the unemployment statistics, and when you are hired, work hard and do your best so you can keep that position.

Interview Time

Let's say you've applied at a business that you'd really like to work for. For Travis, it was a local high-end grocery market that was locally owned. It appealed to him because he knew it was locally owned and that the owners were local. He felt he could make some lasting relationships with those who actually lived in his community.

After he applied, he received an invitation to come to the manager's office for an interview appointment. He was nervous and excited—all at once. He turned to his father, and to Craig, for much-needed advice. Here's what he came up with:

- Put confidence in your step—don't shuffle

- Stand up straight and look people in the eyes

- Smile

- Remember names, and address the interviewer by name

- Answer with more than a *yes* or a *no*. Explain what you mean.

- Don't let nervousness do you in—it's natural and to be expected

More About Job Interviews

The new experience of a job interview can be a little nerve-wracking for a teen. The key is to be as fully prepared as possible before the interview. The fact that you've been granted an interview is a plus to begin with. Not every candidate who applies gets an interview. But what are some of the things you should know, and do, and *not do*?

Learn About the Company

Having the Internet at your fingertips (quite literally) puts you way ahead of those of the generation that came before you. This means you can learn about this company in advance and then share that knowledge during the interview. This research might even give you more respect for this company. That enthusiasm will most certainly come through as you speak to the person conducting the interview.

During the interview, you may very well be asked such things as:

"Why do you want to work here?"

Or

"What do you know about our company?"

What You Can Learn About the Company

What bits of information might serve you well for your interview? Consider the list below:

- The company's motto or logo or both
- The company's mission statement
- Their products—what they're best known for
- Recent news events—what puts them in the news?

As you are doing your research, begin to formulate questions that you might ask the interviewer. Let your knowledge and your interest be apparent.

Learn About the Position

What about the position you're applying for? Check out the company's website in order to learn as much as you can about that position and what all it entails. If you're not clear on exactly what the job entails, ask questions.

If possible, talk to someone who has worked there, or is currently working there. With this background information you'll be that much more aware of what skills you can offer to this position.

Your Resume

As a teen, your resume may be a little *thin,* but don't worry about that. Provide real, solid examples of successes you've had at school, in sports, in clubs, or in other extracurricular activities. Such involvement shows:

- Teamwork

- Organizational skills

- Problem-solving abilities

- Commitment

- Dedication

- Persistence

The Interview

"You never get a second chance to make a first impression."

Ever hear that statement before? Perhaps your parents have said it, or a grandparent. It's not just a cliché; and never is it more applicable than in a job interview. The way you come across in those first few minutes could make the difference between getting the job–or not.

When deciding what to wear, a good rule of thumb is to *over-dress.* This doesn't mean flashy, but professional

For the girls: no midriff showing, exposed shoulders or cleavage. Leave flashy jewelry for the party. Keep make-up moderate.

For the guys: slacks, button-up shirt, possibly a tie depending on the company.

When you look good, you *feel* good; when you feel good you exude confidence.

Now let's look at a few more great tips:

Don't:

- Bring your cell phone (if you do, have it hidden and on silent)
- Chew gum (never ever!)
- Show up hungry (remember how embarrassing it can be to have your stomach rumbling)
- Slouch
- Bring a friend
- Yawn
- Share too much of your personal information

Do:

- Be well rested
- Arrive about five minutes before the appointed time
- Overdress (no jeans, t-shirts, flip-flops, etc.–for girls, modesty is the key)
- Stand up straight; sit up straight

- Bring a file folder containing you resume and paper to take notes (don't forget a pen)

- Shake hands with the interviewer when arriving and leaving

- Follow the interviewer's lead—let him/her point you to a chair

- Maintain eye contact during the interview

- Don't forget to smile!

- Thank them for their time

After the Interview

Always follow up with a thank you email. This will put you way ahead of most all others who are applying.

In this email, you will thank them again for their time. It's at this point that you let them know you are 1) very interested in this position, or 2) now that you've had a closer look, you can see it's not for you. Either way, let them know.

If you have not heard back, and if no date was set for a follow up, check back in about a week to see whether or not the position has been filled.

The interview skills you acquire as a teenager will serve you well in later years when you will be applying for a major career position. Learn all you can while you're young!

. . . . . ● . . . . .

With Craig's help, Travis was able to not only thoroughly fill the application for a position at Lester's, but also put together a professional-looking resume.

"It looks sorta skimpy," Travis said, as he looked over the completed resume.

"Look at it this way," Craig told him. "It's not like the manager of Lester's is looking for a career-veteran stock boy."

Travis laughed at that remark. "No, I guess not."

"He realizes he's dealing with a teen who's looking for a job. He'll be impressed that you cared enough to create a resume at all."

"I hope you're right."

CHAPTER 3

FIRST JOB

Travis tapped Craig's number on his cell phone. "Craig, you gotta come help me."

"Now what. You got the job, right? I thought you'd be out celebrating!"

Travis looked at the pile of papers on his desk. "Maybe later. Right now I have a ton of forms to fill out. What the heck is all this stuff?"

Craig's laugh sounded so loud over the phone, Travis had to hold it away from his ear. "Oh yeah. You have some decisions to make, and legal matters to tend to."

"Do you understand any of this? If so, come over and be my translator."

"Be right there."

. . . . . • ● • . . . .

Congratulations Are in Order

Congratulations! You have just landed your first real job. This is a big step in your life. Sure, you will want to celebrate, but not too much. You now have a job to do! When you find a job, you will be expected to provide proof of your identity. (This was discussed in Chapter 1.) Proof of identity might include your birth certificate, driver's license, a passport, but definitely your Social Security number which is used to track your future income and paid taxes. (That will be explained in the next chapter.)

Learning and performing on the job is not what this chapter is all about. You're on your own in that department. I'll just say you should do your best—and even when you are given tasks that are not your favorite thing to do, maintain a good attitude. Whiners get nowhere in the workaday world. Keep in mind that you have two ears and one mouth—use them proportionately to learn. And last, but not least, always respect authority.

Background Check

At some point in your career (either for your first job, or one later in life as you are promoted, or as you change companies), you will be subject to a criminal history background check and drug screening.

Having a history of crime or experimenting with drugs can ruin your life—so don't do it! It's not worth it. However, if you have made mistakes, or experimented with drugs and been caught, it is not the end of the world. If all that has been put behind you, you will still be able to find a job. You may just need a chance to prove yourself and your accountability. My point here is, if you haven't already put yourself at risk of being turned down for a job, then don't even take the chance.

Forms and More Forms

Assuming you are successful in passing the criminal background check and drug screening, you are then officially hired. As you start your job, there will be numerous forms to fill out, documents to be signed (some of these are to protect the company), and benefit options from which you will have to choose. We'll go over some of the most common forms, documents and benefit options that you'll need to complete throughout your career each time you change employers.

W-4 Form

Whenever you earn wages through employment, you will need to fill out a W-4 form. Here's what one looks like: https://www.irs.gov/pub/irs-pdf/fw4.pdf.

Don't bother with the questions at the top, just go straight to the bottom part where you will fill out your name and address. Check the box that you are single. On line 5, you are going to write "0" exemptions. If this is your first job ever and you're only going to work over the summer and you are positive that you won't make over $5,600 for the entire year, then write the word "exempt" on line seven. That means you're indicating that you don't want any federal income tax withheld. If you want to get a refund next April, then don't write exempt, just keep the "0" on line 5 so there will be withholding. (Many people prefer to have the money in hand rather than letting the government take it and hold it for several months.)

W-9 Form

A W-9 Form is a common Internal Revenue Service (IRS) document. If you were hired by someone as a regular employee or independent contractor, you will fill out a W-9 Form and submit the form to your client or employer. Employers and clients use this information to report your earnings to the IRS and to provide you with a 1099 Form at the end of the year. A 1099 Form shows how much money you made and how much money was deducted in order for you to calculate your income taxes (discussed in a later chapter).

A **W-9 Form** looks like this:

Form **W-9** (Rev. December 2014) Department of the Treasury Internal Revenue Service	**Request for Taxpayer Identification Number and Certification**	Give Form to the requester. Do not send to the IRS.

1 Name (as shown on your income tax return). Name is required on this line; do not leave this line blank.

2 Business name/disregarded entity name, if different from above

3 Check appropriate box for federal tax classification; check only **one** of the following seven boxes:
- [ ] Individual/sole proprietor or single-member LLC
- [ ] C Corporation
- [ ] S Corporation
- [ ] Partnership
- [ ] Trust/estate
- [ ] Limited liability company. Enter the tax classification (C=C corporation, S=S corporation, P=partnership) ▶
- Note. For a single-member LLC that is disregarded, do not check LLC; check the appropriate box in the line above for the tax classification of the single-member owner.
- [ ] Other (see instructions) ▶

4 Exemptions (codes apply only to certain entities, not individuals; see instructions on page 3):
Exempt payee code (if any)
Exemption from FATCA reporting code (if any)
(Applies to accounts maintained outside the U.S.)

5 Address (number, street, and apt. or suite no.)

Requester's name and address (optional)

6 City, state, and ZIP code

7 List account number(s) here (optional)

Print or type. See Specific Instructions on page 2.

Part I Taxpayer Identification Number (TIN)

Enter your TIN in the appropriate box. The TIN provided must match the name given on line 1 to avoid backup withholding. For individuals, this is generally your social security number (SSN). However, for a resident alien, sole proprietor, or disregarded entity, see the Part I instructions on page 3. For other entities, it is your employer identification number (EIN). If you do not have a number, see How to get a TIN on page 3.

Note. If the account is in more than one name, see the instructions for line 1 and the chart on page 4 for guidelines on whose number to enter.

Social security number

or

Employer identification number

Part II Certification

Under penalties of perjury, I certify that:

1. The number shown on this form is my correct taxpayer identification number (or I am waiting for a number to be issued to me); and
2. I am not subject to backup withholding because: (a) I am exempt from backup withholding, or (b) I have not been notified by the Internal Revenue Service (IRS) that I am subject to backup withholding as a result of a failure to report all interest or dividends, or (c) the IRS has notified me that I am no longer subject to backup withholding; and
3. I am a U.S. citizen or other U.S. person (defined below); and
4. The FATCA code(s) entered on this form (if any) indicating that I am exempt from FATCA reporting is correct.

Certification instructions. You must cross out item 2 above if you have been notified by the IRS that you are currently subject to backup withholding because you have failed to report all interest and dividends on your tax return. For real estate transactions, item 2 does not apply. For mortgage interest paid, acquisition or abandonment of secured property, cancellation of debt, contributions to an individual retirement arrangement (IRA), and generally, payments other than interest and dividends, you are not required to sign the certification, but you must provide your correct TIN. See the instructions on page 3.

Sign Here Signature of U.S. person ▶ Date ▶

General Instructions

Section references are to the Internal Revenue Code unless otherwise noted.

Future developments. Information about developments affecting Form W-9 (such as legislation enacted after we release it) is at www.irs.gov/fw9.

Purpose of Form

An individual or entity (Form W-9 requester) who is required to file an information return with the IRS must obtain your correct taxpayer identification number (TIN) which may be your social security number (SSN), individual taxpayer identification number (ITIN), adoption taxpayer identification number (ATIN), or employer identification number (EIN), to report on an information return the amount paid to you, or other amount reportable on an information return. Examples of information returns include, but are not limited to, the following:

- Form 1099-INT (interest earned or paid)
- Form 1099-DIV (dividends, including those from stocks or mutual funds)
- Form 1099-MISC (various types of income, prizes, awards, or gross proceeds)
- Form 1099-B (stock or mutual fund sales and certain other transactions by brokers)
- Form 1099-S (proceeds from real estate transactions)
- Form 1099-K (merchant card and third party network transactions)

- Form 1098 (home mortgage interest), 1098-E (student loan interest), 1098-T (tuition)
- Form 1099-C (canceled debt)
- Form 1099-A (acquisition or abandonment of secured property)

Use Form W-9 only if you are a U.S. person (including a resident alien), to provide your correct TIN.

If you do not return Form W-9 to the requester with a TIN, you might be subject to backup withholding. See What is backup withholding? on page 2.

By signing the filled-out form, you:

1. Certify that the TIN you are giving is correct (or you are waiting for a number to be issued),
2. Certify that you are not subject to backup withholding, or
3. Claim exemption from backup withholding if you are a U.S. exempt payee. If applicable, you are also certifying that as a U.S. person, your allocable share of any partnership income from a U.S. trade or business is not subject to the withholding tax on foreign partners' share of effectively connected income, and
4. Certify that FATCA code(s) entered on this form (if any) indicating that you are exempt from the FATCA reporting, is correct. See What is FATCA reporting? on page 2 for further information.

Cat. No. 10231X   Form **W-9** (Rev. 12-2014)

Make sure you have the right form. If you are the one being hired, then your employer is responsible for giving you the form. Anyone you work for who hires freelancers or independent contractors to work for them, also needs to provide a W-9. You can access the correct W-9 form on the IRS website.

Information for completing this form can be found by going to: http://www.wikihow.com/Complete-a-W9-Tax-Form.

Before you sign and date the form, make sure you read over the completed form and check to see if everything is correct. Read through the "Certification" information in Part II as well, so you know what you're signing off on. Only sign if everything is accurate.

If everything is correct and you have finished reading the certification information, sign your legal name and include the date. (Keep in mind, if you sign the document, and one or more of these statements is false, you could face criminal charges, including perjury.)

The person or company that gave you the W-9 will use it at tax time. The W-9 is for whoever will be paying you for the services rendered. It's not necessary for you to send a copy of the form to the IRS, but you will want to keep a copy for your own records.

Employee Handbook

An employee handbook is a compilation of the policies, procedures, working conditions, and behavioral expectations that guide employee actions in a particular workplace. These policies and procedures range from how to access your employee personnel file, to your open-door policy, your promotion policy, Americans with Disabilities Act (ADA) and Equal Employment Opportunity Commission (EEOC) policies.

Employee handbooks generally include information about the company; a welcome letter from the president or CEO; the company's mission, vision, purpose, values, and broad strategic goals; the company's commitment to employees; and various non-compete, non-disclosure, and employee confidentiality agreements, if the company uses them.

They also summarize attendance expectations, define nonexempt and exempt employment statuses, cover severe weather closings, the use of company property, and anything else employees need to know.

Finally, most handbooks clearly present employee compensation and benefits, plus paid time off in detail, and additional terms and conditions of employment.

Non-Compete and Non-Solicitation

In industries where customer lists are essential, the employer will often seek to prevent an employee from "stealing" clients through the use of legal covenants, namely the non-competition (non-compete) and non-solicitation agreements.

The restrictiveness of non-compete and non-solicitation agreements determines whether the contract will be enforced in court. A non-compete agreement bars a former employee from competing against a former employer for a specified amount of time. If the employee, for example, had worked in a pharmaceutical company, a non-compete agreement would prevent him or her from working in the pharmaceutical industry. Oftentimes, these agreements are restricted to a specific geographic area.

The non-solicitation agreement is a less restrictive contract and is narrowly aimed at preventing an employee from soliciting his or her former employer's clients. Unlike the non-compete agreement, the employee is allowed to immediately start work in the same industry and in the same geographic area.

www.burkelaw.com/pressroom-114.html

Non-Disclosure and Confidentiality Agreement

Have you ever been asked to keep a secret? If so, you probably took great measures to keep that information to yourself, simply out of respect for the person who passed along the private information. A confidentiality agreement, also called a *nondisclosure agreement* or *NDA*, takes this idea of keeping a secret a step further. This contract creates a legal obligation to privacy and compels those who agree to keep any specified information top-secret or secured.

NDAs are fairly common in many business settings, as they offer one of the most surefire ways to protect trade secrets and other confidential information meant to be kept under wraps. Information commonly protected by NDAs might include schematics for a new product, client information, sales and marketing plans, or a unique manufacturing process. Using a nondisclosure agreement means the company's secrets will be protected, and if not, the company will have legal recourse and might even be able to sue for damages.

Confidentiality agreements typically serve three key functions:

1. NDAs protect sensitive information. By signing an NDA, participants promise to not divulge or release information shared with them by the other people involved. If the information is leaked, the injured person can claim breach of contract.

2. In the case of new product or concept development, a confidentiality agreement can help the inventor keep patent rights. In many cases, public disclosure of a new invention can void patent rights. A properly drafted NDA can help the original creator hold onto the rights to a product or idea.

3. Confidentiality agreements and NDAs expressly outline what information is private and what's fair game. In

many cases, the agreement serves as a document that classifies exclusive and confidential information.

Money Choices

Once money begins to come your direction, there will be a multitude of decisions that will present themselves. Some people have the mistaken notion that money is the answer to everything. Bad thinking. It's never a matter of how much money you have, it's all about *what you do with the money you have.* (This admonition will be repeated several times within this book–it's crucial to grasp the concept.)

A classic example is the *King of Pop,* Michael Jackson. When he died in 2009, he was about *$400 million in debt.* Hundreds of millions in debt? How could that be? I won't go into detail here, but it all came down to what Michael Jackson chose to do with the money that came to him. Quite simply, he just made a lot of bad money-management decisions.

401K Plan

One of the choices that may be given to you when you start work will be to sign up for the company's 401K Plan. If I tell you this can help with your future retirement, you'll probably roll your eyes and heave a big sigh. Long, long time until you will be thinking about retirement, right?

But what if instead of retirement, I told you that this is a great way to not only save money, but to *grow* money. (Did you know that money can grow? Many teens don't know. We'll discuss this in a later chapter.)

Let's take a closer look at the 401k plan. Simply put, a 401k is a way for you as an employee to contribute money to an account, most often pre-tax. You can choose different plans and options to invest your money, and in many cases, your employer will match the funds you put into your account.

Did you get that? You choose to put money from your earnings into this account, and the company will contribute money to your plan. In other words, your money is growing without you having to do any extra work.

When you sign up for your company's 401k plan you will decide how much of your paycheck to direct-deposit into the retirement account. You can choose a percentage or fixed-dollar amount to be deducted each month and invested into this account. This seemingly simple decision could have an enormous impact on how prepared you are for future financial security.

A good strategy is to start out saving a very small percentage of pay, such as 1 percent, and increase it each time you get a raise. A portion of windfalls of cash such as bonuses, tax refunds, or gifts, can also be redirected to your retirement account.

A financial adviser should be able to help you calculate how much you need to save each year to achieve your desired retirement lifestyle. On average, 401k plan sponsors say employees should be saving at least 12% of their pay, including employer contributions, over their entire working career in order to provide adequate income during retirement. (This is according to a Principal Financial Group online survey conducted by Harris Interactive.)

A little piece of advice here—do not withdraw money from your retirement account throughout your career, as there will be large financial consequences. As you look out across the years–through your working/career years–it's important to plan for enjoying a high level quality of life when you are older, or if you are unable to work due to disability, or if you choose to stop working because you have reached retirement age. How nice it would be to be able to live the rest of your life without working.

When you think about working to make money, think about saving for your retirement, and never separate the two. Accept the fact that you will make money, pay taxes, contribute to your retirement—that's a given. The money that's left in your paycheck is yours to make other decisions about. Never fail to save for your retirement with every paycheck received, and as you make more money, make larger contributions proportionately.

Fidelity Investments

Fidelity (https://www.fidelity.com/) can provide a lot of information for you and is a very popular choice for employers to offer their employees. When you change jobs and companies, your new employer will set up another retirement account for you to contribute to. The money can get "rolled together" in one retirement institute to help keep all your money with one company. I recommend Fidelity Investments for everyone. The company is very well established; and even though there may be others, you won't go wrong with this one. You will have online access to your account to monitor balances and select investments for yourself.

Health/Medical, Dental and Vision Insurance

Health insurance is a type of insurance coverage that covers the cost of an insured individual's medical and surgical expenses. Depending on the type of health insurance coverage, either the insured pays costs out-of-pocket and is then reimbursed, or the insurer makes payments directly to the provider.

In health insurance terminology, the "provider" is a clinic, hospital, doctor, laboratory, health care practitioner, or pharmacy. The "insured" is the owner of the health insurance policy—the person with the health insurance coverage.

Everybody at some time in their life, and often on many occasions, will need some kind of medical attention and treatment. When medical care is required, ideally, the patient should be able to concentrate on getting better, rather than wondering whether he/she has the resources to pay for all the bills. This view is becoming more commonly held in nearly all the developed nations.

Employers in the United States with more than 50 employees are required to offer employee healthcare benefits. Simultaneously, the employer also looks into offering their employees basic dental insurance coverage for you to have annual checkups and cleanings and also vision insurance, which benefits people who wear glasses or contact lenses.

My recommendation is to think about the possibility of a catastrophic-type of event, such as a car wreck (which is exactly what happened to me), or a major health issue that could arise. If you have no insurance, you may end up in debt for the rest of your life, so make sure the cost of any hospital stay is minimized with sufficient coverage.

Two Main Plans

There are two main plans offered to you–an HMO or a PPO. The table on the following page explains the difference:

	HMO Health Maintenance Organization	PPO Preferred Provider Organization
Do I need to designate a Primary Care Physician (PCP)?	**YES** With most HMO plans, all of your healthcare services will be coordinated between you and your designated Primary Care Physician (PCP).	**NO** A PPO plan does not require you to select a PCP. You can receive care from any doctor you choose, however you will save more money by choosing a doctor, specialist or hospital that is within your network.
Is a referral needed?	**YES** As an example, with an HMO, if you have severe allergies and need to see an allergist, you will first schedule a visit with your PCP. Your doctor will then provide you with a referral for an in-network specialist.	**NO** PPO plans do not require you to get a referral in order to see a specialist.
If I have a doctor or specialist who is out-of-network, will I still be able to see them and have my care covered?	**NO** HMOs don't offer coverage for care from an out-of-network physician, hospital or facility except in the case of a true medical emergency.	**YES** With a PPO, you have the flexibility to visit providers, hospitals and facilities outside of your network. Keep in mind that visiting an out-of-network provider includes a higher fee and a separate deductible.
Will I have to file a claim?	**NO** Since HMOs only allow you to see in-network providers, it's likely you'll never have to file a claim. This is because your insurance company pays the provider directly.	**YES** In some cases with a PPO, you will have to pay a doctor for services directly and then file a claim to get reimbursed. This is most common when you seek a service from an out-of-network provider.
How much will it cost?	**Lower Cost** HMO plans typically have lower monthly premiums and you can expect to pay less for out-of-pocket medical services. Both plans work on a combination of deductibles, cost-share or co-insurance and co-pays to pay for services.	**Higher Cost** PPOs tend to have higher monthly premiums in exchange for the flexibility to choose providers both in- and out-of-network and without a referral. Out-of-pocket medical costs can also run higher with a PPO plan.

Find out if your doctor is on the list of HMO service providers. Assuming you do not have any major health concerns and your doctor is listed in the HMO, then choose the best plan for you based on your health and the price. Do not assume the most expensive insurance plan is the best for you. Read what each plan offers and make a decision based on your own health condition.

Having health insurance is required by law. It will be a deduction from your paycheck. Think of this as a way of reducing your expenses when you do get ill, and you will. It is just a matter of time before you will need medical attention, so financially protect yourself when you can and as much as you can.

Short-Term and Long-Term Disability Insurance

Disability insurance is private insurance that replaces some of your income if an injury or illness prevents you from working. This type of insurance is important because it can ease the financial burden on a household when someone has a serious illness or injury.

There are two types of disability insurance:

- Short-Term Disability (STD) pays you a portion of your income for a short period of time after you run out of sick leave. Depending on your plan, STD will generally pay for between 9 and 52 weeks (or 1 year).

- Long-Term Disability (LTD) pays you a portion of your income after you run out of both sick leave and STD. Depending on your plan, LTD may pay you for a specific number of years, like 2 to 5 years, or until you turn a specific age, like 65.

Life Insurance

A life insurance policy is a contract with an insurance

company. In exchange for premium payments, the insurance company provides a lump-sum payment, known as a death benefit, to beneficiaries upon the insured's death.

Typically, life insurance is chosen based on the needs and goals of the owner. Term life insurance generally provides protection for a set period of time, while permanent insurance, such as whole and universal life, provides lifetime coverage. It's important to note that death benefits from all types of life insurance are generally income-tax free.

There are many varieties of life insurance. Some of the more common types are discussed below.

Term Life Insurance

Term life insurance is designed to provide financial protection for a specific period of time, such as 10 or 20 years. With traditional term insurance, the premium payment amount stays the same for the coverage period you select. After that period, policies may offer continued coverage, usually at a substantially higher premium payment rate. Term life insurance is generally less expensive than permanent life insurance.

Needs It Helps Meet

Term life insurance proceeds can be used to replace lost potential income during working years. This can provide a safety net for your beneficiaries and can also help ensure the family's financial goals will still be met—goals like paying off a mortgage, keeping a business running, and paying for college.

It's important to note that, although term life can be used to replace lost potential income, life insurance benefits are paid at one time in a lump sum, not in regular payments like paychecks.

Universal Life Insurance

Universal life insurance is a type of permanent life insurance designed to provide lifetime coverage. Unlike whole life insurance, universal life insurance policies are flexible and may allow you to raise or lower your premium payment or coverage amounts throughout your lifetime. Additionally, due to its lifetime coverage, universal life typically has higher premium payments than term.

Needs It Helps Meet

Universal life insurance is most often used as part of a flexible estate planning strategy to help preserve wealth to be transferred to beneficiaries. Another common use is long-term income replacement, where the need extends beyond working years. Some universal life insurance products focus on providing both death benefit coverage and building cash value, while others focus on providing guaranteed death benefit coverage.

Whole Life Insurance

Whole life insurance is a type of permanent life insurance designed to provide lifetime coverage. Because of the lifetime coverage period, whole life usually has higher premium payments than term life. Policy premium payments are typically fixed, and, unlike term, whole life has a cash value, which functions as a savings component and may accumulate tax-deferred over time.

Needs It Helps Meet

Whole life can be used as an estate-planning tool to help preserve the wealth you plan to transfer to your beneficiaries.

Not an Investment

A life insurance policy is not an investment. It is designed to protect your family in the event you die unexpectedly by giving them cash for future needs in life. It is also a way for you to protect your assets and investments until you reach retirement and have enough money saved. I suggest a 30+-year term policy starting as soon as possible to keep the cost down and then focusing the rest of your career on saving enough money until the policy becomes null and void.

· · · · **·** **●** **·** · · ·

Travis focused intently on his task at hand–taking apples from the packing boxes and arranging them neatly in the produce display. He didn't even notice Joey until his cousin was standing right next to him. Then it startled him.

"Scare a guy out of his wits, why don't you?" Travis said, somewhat annoyed.

"Man, you're really into the apples, aren't you?" Joey said.

"I just want to do the job right. So what brings you to Lester's Foods? I would hardly believe you're now doing the family grocery shopping."

"Not a chance."

Joey paused a minute till Travis looked over at him. Travis knew that look. It was Joey's I'm-about-to-ask-you-for-something look.

"Okay. So what's up?"

"I've been thinking. Maybe I should earn some cash while I'm investigating these online businesses."

Travis tapped his ear. "Is there an echo in here? I think I heard someone say that very thing recently."

Joey ignored the remark. "Trav, are there any openings here for another stocker?"

Travis stopped arranging apples. "No, Joey. No more openings. But hey, why would you want to work here anyway? You don't even like grocery stores—except to eat what comes from here."

"Well I just thought…"

"Look, why don't you think of what you *really* like."

"Such as?"

"You love movies, right?"

"Absolutely."

"So. How many movie theaters are there in this town?"

"A bunch."

"Go put your applications in there. You'd love it. You'd have the scoop on every new release."

Joey snapped his fingers. "Wow! Hey, Trav, that's a great idea. Why didn't I think of that?"

"You were too busy looking for easy money online."

"I could see more movies, and write up more movie reviews on my blog." Joey turned to go. "Hey, maybe employees even get free popcorn."

Travis had to laugh. His cousin was a hoot. "Maybe. Now I gotta get back to work. They aren't paying me to stand around, you know."

· · · · ● · · · ·

First the job, then the paycheck—oh happy day! If that's true, then why is Joey so glum? Let's drop in and find out.

CHAPTER 4

BETTER YET, FIRST PAYCHECK

After Travis got off work on Saturday, he stopped by Joey's house. He knew his cousin was due to have his first paycheck in hand, and expected Joey would want to go get pizza or something to celebrate.

When he pulled up in the drive (his dad had let him use the car again), Joey was sitting on the front step looking bummed.

Travis got out and walked over to where Joey was sitting. "What's with the long face, Cuz? I thought you'd be over here doing double back flips. You just got paid, didn't you? Your very first paycheck?"

"Oh yeah. I got paid all right. And they cheated me! The theater cheated me on my pay. I thought they liked my work, everybody's cool about my performance on the job." He looked up at Travis. "So why would they cheat me?"

Travis sat down on the front porch step beside Joey. "What the heck are you talking about. How do you think you were cheated?"

"I had it all figured out in my head. You know, keeping track of my hours and all that. And they gave me a lot of hours my first two weeks."

"So?"

"So! What I got paid was way less than what I had calculated."

"Joey, there're certain things that are deducted from your check, and will be each pay period. Where's your stub?"

"My what?"

"The check stub. That part that you detached from your paycheck before you cashed it."

"Oh, that thing. I think it's upstairs on my desk."

"Go get it."

"Now?"

"Now—if you want to understand exactly how you are paid."

The door slammed as Joey went inside. In a moment, he was back with the slip of paper in hand.

Travis took it from him, then asked, "Is your dad home?"

"He's in the living room."

"C'mon. Let's go get an expert to decipher this."

· · · · • ● ● • · · ·

Paycheck Deductions

Opening your own checking account is a good way to keep your money under control, and to keep the cash out of your hands where there's so much more temptation to spend it.

But before we get into a discussion about banks and checking accounts, let's take a long, hard look at the paycheck that you plan to deposit into that account.

If you're like most people, your paycheck means only one thing–money in the bank! But if you find yourself existing paycheck to paycheck, and running out of money before the next pay period comes around, you probably need to improve your money management skills. You need to pay close attention to that *other* portion of your paycheck known as the paycheck stub (the part that Joey had failed to read).

It's important that you know how to read that pay stub and understand the information it contains. This information plays an important role in effective money management and good budgeting. Knowing where your money is going can help you stay on top of your finances and make the most of your hard-earned paycheck.

	MAY 15	Whole Foods	Groceries		-$56.09
	MAY 15	Starbucks	Coffee Shops		-$3.27
	MAY 15	Amazon	Shopping	▼	-$41.99

DETAILS	Appears on your ABC Bank statement as **AMAZON.COM** AMZN.COM08/28C on May 15	SPLIT

TAGS	☐ Reimbursable ☐ Spouse		
	Manage your tags	Cancel	I'm Done

What is Included on a Paycheck Stub?

As you can see from the graphic above, a number of items are listed that have been deducted from this paycheck. Some of these items showed up on Joey's check as well, and this is what he needed his father to explain.

Although every company prints paychecks that are unique to that company, there are some aspects of the employee paycheck that, by law, employers must include. Some paycheck stubs can be extremely detailed including such items as retirement plan contributions, or accrued vacation time, and others will only detail the required information. The following items will appear on every paycheck stub and employees need to know their definitions and value:

- **Gross Pay:** Includes the total amount of income that you earned during a particular pay period. A pay period is determined by your employer, but is typically bi-weekly or monthly. This figure does not factor in tax withholdings.

- **Net Pay:** Includes the amount of income that you actually take home after all withholdings have been applied. It is the amount of money that you take to the bank!

- **Federal Tax Amount:** When you were first hired by your employer, you were required to fill out a W-4 form. (See Chapter 3.) This form covers any tax that you may owe to the Federal Government when you file your Income Taxes at the end of the year. It is deducted incrementally from each paycheck, and can vary depending on the number of exemptions you chose to claim.

- **State Tax:** Depending on your state of residence,

you may or may not be required to pay a state tax. Most states, however, do participate in requiring state taxes, so this amount is deducted from your paycheck (the same way as Federal tax) to cover the amount of tax that you may owe to the state when your tax return is filed.

- **Social Security:** The Federal Government requires every employee to have a certain percentage of their paycheck withheld for Social Security purposes. This entitles you to receive a monthly Social Security payment upon retirement.

- **Medicare:** Like Social Security withholdings, Medicare withholdings are also mandatory. Every employee pays 1.45% of their paycheck toward Medicare, and every employer contributes an additional 1.45% on behalf of the employee. Upon eligibility for Social Security, an employee is entitled to coverage for a majority of their medical expenses.

- **Year-to-date (for pay and deductions):** The year-to-date fields on your paycheck stub show how much you have paid toward a particular withholding at any point in the calendar year. This can be useful when budgeting for monthly expenses or long-term goals.

Although not required, the following are items that may appear on your paycheck stub and are useful to money management and relevant to your employment status.

- **Insurance Deductions:** Monthly payments for such types of insurance as health (medical and dental), and life insurance.

- **Retirement Plan Contributions:** Plans such as 401k or 403b retirement savings plans.

- **Leave Time:** Including vacation hours or sick hours.

Most employers will detail how many hours have been used to date, and how many hours are remaining for the calendar year.

- **Childcare Assistance:** If offered by your employer, this amount may appear on each paycheck as a pre-tax benefit.

- **Important Notices:** Employers often use a portion of the paycheck stub to communicate important pieces of information to their employees such as wage increases or notifications about tax filings.

Common Abbreviations Used on Paycheck Stubs

- **YTD:** Year-to-Date

- **FT or FWT:** Federal Tax or Federal Withholding Tax

- **ST or SWT:** State Tax or State Withholding Tax

- **SS or SSWT:** Social Security or Social Security Withholding Tax

- **MWT or Med:** Medicare Withholding Tax

If you need further explanation on how to read your paycheck stub, or if a particular calculation doesn't seem correct, consult your Human Resources Department for assistance. Don't procrastinate! Exercise good money management skills by being proactive. If a calculation is incorrect, the issue may reappear on every paycheck. Also, you may not be making the best choice for a retirement plan contribution, or losing money, if your earnings are not calculated properly. It is ultimately *your responsibility* to ensure that you are being properly compensated.

(Information based on this site: http://www.clearpoint.org/how-to-read-your-pay-stub)

Depositing Your Check

When you receive a paycheck, you can take it to your bank and make a deposit into your account. Or, instead of receiving a "live check" and the inconvenience of driving to your bank to make the deposit, you can request your employer to make a direct deposit into your bank account for you.

In banking, a direct deposit (or direct credit) is a deposit of money by a payer directly into a payee's bank account. Direct deposits are most commonly made by businesses in the payment of salaries and wages. These deposits are made by means of electronic funds transfers effected using online, mobile, and telephone banking systems.

When making a direct deposit by means of electronic funds transfer, the payer would also normally enter reference information to enable the payee to easily recognize who made the deposit and which account to credit. The reference may be an account number, an invoice number, the payer's name, or some other meaningful identification. To ensure that the payee is aware of the deposit, the payer would commonly follow up by sending to the payee a remittance advice or copy of paystub.

https://en.wikipedia.org/wiki/Direct_deposit

Now that you know more about your paycheck and how your pay is computed, let's turn our attention to the subject of banks and banking.

CHAPTER 5

MONEY IN THE BANK

The water created a rainbow as Travis sprayed the soap off his dad's car. His dad had let him use it a couple times, and the deal was Travis would keep it washed and vacuumed in exchange for the privileges.

Ever since Joey started working at the movie theater, he'd been a little scarce. So Travis was surprised to see his cousin come barreling down the street on his dirt bike. He was waving something in his hand. He screeched the bike to a stop inches from where Travis was standing.

"Better look out if you don't want a shower," Travis warned, waving the spray nozzle in Joey's direction.

"That's no threat. It'd feel good on a day like this."

"So why are you riding ninety-to-nothing in this heat?"

"Had to show you–this!"

Travis laid down the hose, turned off the water, dried his hands, and took what Joey was waving about in the air.

"It's a checkbook."

"Well duh. Smart you are, Cuz."

"So? What's the big deal?"

"I have a checking account. This is MY checkbook."

"You're kidding." Travis opened the checkbook to see his cousin's name and address on the checks inside. Travis had been thinking of opening an account himself, but just hadn't gotten around to it. "Good for you, Joey. This is great."

"Yeah. For once I got one-up on you."

"You sure did." Just then a text message came through and Travis pulled his phone from his back pocket. It was from Craig. Travis read it and laughed. "It's from your brother," he told Joey.

"So what does he want?"

Travis handed over the phone so Joey could see. The message said:

"Have you seen Joey? Did he tell you that Mom dragged him to the bank today and made him open a checking account?"

A sheepish look came over Joey's face. He handed the phone back. "Well, I was going to open one anyway. Mom just got in a hurry."

"Sure you were."

"Hey, I'll help you finish up here. Then we can go to the bank and I'll show you how to open your account."

"Joey, you're too good to me."

. . . . . ● . . . .

An Important Step

For a teenager just beginning to establish his or her financial life, opening a checking account is a small, but important, step in that process. A checking account is the workhorse of your accounts. It's for money that you plan on spending or transferring to another account quickly. Because of the ease with which you can deposit and withdraw from a checking account, it will likely be the hub of all your financial activity.

Below are a few important tips on opening your first checking account. (While you're at it, open up a savings account, too, for your emergency fund.) For those of you who already have a checking account, here are a few reminders on managing it wisely.

What to Look for in a Checking Account

Not all checking accounts are created equal. Some banks offer higher than average interest rates, while others offer accounts that pay no interest. Some banks charge a monthly fee to keep your money with them, while others offer free checking accounts. Below are a few things to consider when selecting and applying for a checking account.

Free Checking Accounts

Look for free checking accounts, but understand that a free checking account isn't really *free*. A free checking account is an account that doesn't charge you a monthly service fee to keep your money in that account. Many banks used to offer free checking accounts without any strings attached, but those days are largely over. These days, most banks won't charge you a monthly fee *so long as you meet certain conditions*. Usually the conditions are that you make a pre-determined number of direct deposits and debit card transactions each month, or you maintain a certain minimum balance.

If you fail to meet those requirements, the monthly service fee is around $5 at most banks.

No Minimum Balance

When you're young and just starting out in life, your cash flow is likely minuscule. When I was in college, it was common for my checking account to dip below $100 despite my best efforts at budgeting. If you have a bank account that requires a minimum balance and you dip below that number, you're going to be slapped with a penalty. Many free checking accounts have no minimum balance requirement (but require you to make direct deposits or debit card transactions to keep the account free), so select one of those.

Avoid checking accounts that offer higher-than-normal interest rates. They look enticing, but they usually require a minimum balance of a few thousand dollars.

Online Access

You want to keep on top of how much money is coming in and going out of your checking account. It used to be you had to religiously keep track of every single one of your transactions in a paper check register if you wanted to know how much you had in your account. Today most banks offer free online services that let you check your account online. Get one that does. Also check to see if your bank allows you to hook up your accounts with services like Mint (https://www.mint.com/), YouNeedaBudget (https://www.youneedabudget.com/), or Quicken (https://www.quicken.com/). Keeping track of your checkbook on your computer is much easier than using the old pocket register.

Understand Holds

Let's say you get a big fat $2,000 from Grandpa to help pay for school. You deposit it in your account. Now you're ready to drop a $2,000 money bomb at the bursar's office the next day, right? Nope.

Banks usually place *holds* on checks from other banks (especially out-of-state banks), for a few days to ensure the check or electronic deposit will be honored by the issuing bank. During this hold period, you won't have access to the money you deposited. For checks from local sources, the hold period is usually two days; for out-of-state check sources, the hold period can be up to five days.

It's important to know your bank's policy so you don't spend money that you don't have access to yet.

Debit Cards

Most banks offer customers a debit card when they open up an account. Debit cards offer the convenience of credit cards, without the crippling high interest rates. Whenever you swipe a check card, the amount of your purchase is deducted from your checking account. You will want to pay close attention to the use of your debit card as you can easily overdraw on your account.

Choosing Credit or Debit on Check Card Readers

Whenever you swipe your check card at a store, you'll often be asked to select "credit" or "debit." While both options will result in money being deducted from your checking account, they each process the transaction differently.

If you select "credit" and your check card happens to be a Visa checking card, your transaction is verified with your signature (sometimes), and will be processed through Visa's networks. The benefit to you for using your debit card as credit is that you get to take advantage of Visa's added security options to prevent against fraudulent transactions.

You can also earn reward points with certain cards. Store

owners have to pay Visa a pretty hefty service fee (usually 2% of the transaction) every time you choose credit, which is why you may have noticed the check card readers at your favorite store bring up debit as the default option, forcing you to press the cancel button, and select credit instead.

If you select *debit*, you'll need to enter your four-digit PIN. After you enter it, your transaction will be processed through an electronic funds transfer, and funds are taken from your account instantly. You don't get the same protections on your purchase as you do when you select credit, and debit transactions aren't eligible for reward programs.

You can, however, ask for cash back when you make a purchase using debit. That means if your purchase was $5, you can have the store debit your card for $25, and the store will give you $20 straight from the till. That comes in handy when you need cash, but don't want to pay an ATM fee. Be aware that store owners, especially mom and pop places, prefer debit transactions because of the reduced service cost.

ATM Convenience

You'll have those days when you need quick access to cash. That's where ATMs (Automated Teller Machines) will come in handy. But the convenience of ATMs comes at a price. While most banks offer machines that don't charge withdrawal fees for their own customers, banks will charge you a fee for using a competitor's ATM. When you add that fee to the fee or surcharge that the competitor's bank charges you to use their ATM, you're looking at paying about $5 just to get your cash. Always stop and ask yourself: *Is it worth it?*

Online Banking?

In the past few years, the number of online-only banks has increased dramatically. Because they have less overhead than brick-and-mortar banks, online banks are able to provide higher interest rates and charge fewer fees. A few years ago, online banks like ING Direct (https://www.ingdirect.com.au/) and Ally (https://www.ally.com/), had crazy monthly interest rates between 2%-4%, but they've since gone down to about 0.8-1%. Not fantastic, but still better than most traditional banks.

While checking accounts from online banks provide higher interest rates than traditional banks, it's still best to open your first checking account with a traditional bank. Here's why.

Transactions Take Longer

Transactions take longer to clear with online accounts. The internet is supposed to make things faster, but online banks didn't get the memo. Checks and even electronic deposits, however big or small, seem to take forever to clear online banks. For example, when I make transfers from my main checking account to my emergency fund that I keep in an online ING checking account, it takes about three days before I have access to that money. For large deposits or transfers, the wait is longer. Not good if you need money to clear fast.

Can't Deposit Paper or Cash

If you ever get a check or cash for your birthday from Aunt Gertrude, depositing that money into your online banking account can be tricky. Most online banks require all your transactions to be electronic. But there are some that allow you to mail the check or cash. Even if you can mail the paper check, it will be a while before you have access to that money—you have to wait for the check to arrive at the online bank's headquarters, and then you have to wait another couple of days before the check clears.

However, some online banks are beginning to provide

services that allow you to deposit a check from anywhere by simply snapping a photo of the check with your smart-phone, so this is changing.

Many online banks also don't provide wire services or cashier's checks. That can get you into trouble when you're buying a car or a home (or posting bond to get someone out of jail!), as those transactions often require a cashier's check. If all your money is in an online bank on closing day, you're sunk.

Traditional Banks Offer Service

The only customer service you get with online banks comes by phone or email, but there are some issues that are more easily managed face-to-face with a teller. That only happens with a traditional bank. Traditional banks also typically have a network of fee-free ATMs in your area; not so with online banks.

Opening Your Account

Opening a checking account is a breeze. Just walk into the bank and inform the teller that you'd like to open an account. All you have to do is fill out a short application, show the teller your photo ID, and deposit some money to open up an account. The amount you have to initially deposit will vary from bank to bank—some require only $1, while others ask for $50, $100, or even $250.

Some banks even let you open up an account online, but you'll have to have an account at another institution that you can use to fund your new account.

How to Write a Check

Because we don't typically write checks every day, when it comes time to do so, it's easy to mess up. Here's how you do it:

John Doe
123 Main St
Anywhere US 10111

790

Date 01/01/2016

PAY TO THE
ORDER OF THE SANDWICH SHOP $ 8.15

EIGHT AND 15/100   DOLLARS

Your Bank
498 Main St
Anywhere US 10111

MEMO Lunch w/ Friends   Jane Doe

http://banking.about.com/od/howtobank/ss/How-to-Write-a-Check.htm

1. Always date your checks.

2. Write the name of the person or business you're paying next to "Pay to the order of."

3. Write the amount of the check in numeric format. You should start as far over to the left as possible. This prevents anybody from slipping in an extra number or two.

4. Write out the amount of the check in words. For the cents part, use a fraction with 100 as the denominator.

5. Sign the check.

6. It's a good idea to write a short note on what the check was for. It helps with accounting.

Managing Your Checking Account

Now that you have a checking account, it's important that you manage it effectively. If you don't keep on top of the money coming and going from your account, you risk the embarrassment and financial penalties that come from spending money you don't have. If checks start *bouncing* (being returned for insufficient funds), it can get very expensive. These are expenses you don't want to have to pay.

Overdraft Protection

Overdraft protection means that if you make a purchase with your debit card, and you don't have enough money in your account to complete the transaction, the bank will *loan* you the money and charge you a $25-$35 fee for their generosity. That's a big price to pay to avoid the embarrassment or inconvenience of having your card declined or a check bounce. And those fees can add up fast.

Here's what many consumers don't know: most banks will purposefully *process your largest transactions first*, and then your smaller transactions after that. So let's say you have $285 in your checking account, and you buy a coffee for $3.50 in the morning, a sandwich for $5 at noon, and then some college textbooks in the afternoon for $300. The banks will process the $300 transaction *first*, even though it was made later in the day, thus depleting your account, and then charge you a $35 overdraft fee for the textbooks, another $35 fee for the sandwich and another $35 for the coffee, and bill you for $105 in total overdraft fees. Ouch!

Banks used to automatically enroll their customers in overdraft protection programs, but a court ruling in 2010 made that illegal. You can and should opt out of overdraft protection. But because overdraft fees were a big money-maker for banks, they still aggressively try to get you to sign up. Every time I check my bank account online, I get a pop-up that asks if I'm sure I don't want to enroll in their overdraft protection program. I just keep saying no. You should too.

Check Your Account Weekly

Make a habit of checking your account online every week. Not only does this keep you abreast of how much you have in your account so you don't overspend, it gives you a chance to check for errors or fraudulent transactions. If you notice any errors or possible fraudulent transactions, notify your bank immediately.

Also, when you have something set up on autopay, like a gym membership or Netflix that makes a withdrawal from your checking account every month, even when you cancel the service, they can *forget* to stop charging your account. Be on the lookout for this.

Understanding Your Bank Balance

This is something that trips up a lot of young people when they first get a checking account. You log in to your online account and the bank says you have $750 in your checking account, so you write a check for $600 for rent. A few days later you get notice from your bank that you're being charged an overdraft fee and you have a negative account balance. What happened?

A week earlier you wrote a check for $300 for tuition, but it still hadn't cleared when you checked your checking account. After you sent a check to your landlord, the tuition check finally cleared, leaving you in the hole and facing a stiff overdraft fee.

Because of the delay between the moment the transaction occurs and when it actually posts, it's important to track all your debit card transactions, ATM withdrawals, and checks written in a check register. You can use the old-fashioned paper registers that comes with your checkbook, or you can use a digital one like Quicken (http://www.quicken.com), YouNeedABudget (https://www.youneedabudget.com), or Mint (https://www.mint.com). (More about Mint in a later chapter.)

A check register lets you know how much you *really* have available in your account. Don't think you can mentally keep track of it. At some point you'll experience a brain fart. I know from experience.

Set-Up Online Alerts

To play it safe, establish a base amount for your checking account that you'll never go under. That small amount acts like a firewall for bounced checks. Take it a step further by setting up an alert with your bank's online system that will notify you whenever your checking account balance gets within $50 of your minimum balance. Once you get the alert, cut back on spending and deposit some money.

Use Direct Deposit for Paychecks and Pay Bills Online

When you land that job, ask your employer to automatically deposit your paychecks into your checking account. You'll have to sign a form and provide a voided check to get auto-deposits set up. When and where it's available, pay as many of your bills online as you can and make them automatic.

Balance Your Checkbook Monthly

You've probably seen your parents balance their checkbooks. Balancing a checkbook simply means reconciling the balance your bank says you have in your account with the balance you have in your records. Remember, with the delays between checks clearing, those numbers can be off.

(This material was based on information from this site: http://www.artofmanliness.com/2012/08/03/how-to-open-and-manage-a-checking-account/)

How to Balance Your Checkbook in 10 Easy Steps!

1. You will need your check register (where you record your deposits and payments) and your bank statement (to see what has been processed through the bank).

2. In your register, mark off all those items that have

cleared the bank (those that appear on your statement).

3. Use the forms below to calculate the true balance in your account.

4. In the DEPOSITS table, enter the date and amount of all deposits you've made that are not listed on your bank statement. Add the deposits in the Amount column to calculate the Total Deposits that have not cleared the bank.

DEPOSITS		
Date of Deposit		Amount
	+	
	+	
	+	
	+	
Total Deposits	=	

5. In the WITHDRAWALS table, list any checks, ATM withdrawals, store debits, or other automatic withdrawals that have been made, but are not listed on your bank statement.

Make sure to record fees that you anticipate will be charged to your account. Add the withdrawals in the Amount column to calculate the Total Withdrawals that have not cleared the bank.

WITHDRAWALS

Check # or Other Withdrawal		Amount
	+	
	+	
	+	
	+	
	+	
	+	
	+	
	+	
Total Withdrawals	=	

ACCOUNT BALANCE

Enter the ending balance shown on your bank statement		
Add Total Deposits (from DEPOSITS table)	+	
Subtotal	=	
Subtract Total Withdrawals (from WITHDRAWALS table)	−	
The result should equal your true balance.	=	

Note: If you choose to close your bank account, be sure to leave enough money in the account to cover your outstanding checks and other electronic transactions. You should leave at least the amount of Total Withdrawals from the WITHDRAWALS table.

(This material was based on information from this site: https://static1.st8fm.com/en_US/content_pages/1/pdf/us/ checkbook-balance-instructions.pdf)

Savings Accounts

It's a great idea to have a savings account. This way you have a "container" for any surplus you have at the end of the month. Better yet, as you begin to get control of your finances, it's a good idea to have a set amount that you plan to put in your savings account the moment you receive that paycheck.

A savings account is designed to provide an incentive for you to save money. You can make deposits and withdrawals, but can't write checks. They usually pay an interest rate that's higher than a checking account, but lower than a money market account or CD (Certificate of Deposit). Some savings accounts have a passbook, in which transactions are logged in a small booklet that you keep, while others have a monthly or quarterly statement detailing the transactions. Some savings accounts charge a fee if your balance falls below a specified minimum. Check with your bank to make sure.

Understanding the basics of banking is not difficult, but it is necessary. The more you know and understand, the better money manager you will be. And speaking of managing, let's talk about keeping a budget.

CHAPTER 6

BUDGET YOUR MONEY; KNOW WHERE IT GOES

Travis and Joey were leaving their favorite pizza hangout and Travis was annoyed. He'd just watched Joey pay a sizeable tab for several of their friends. Travis was pretty sure the act of benevolence was mainly to impress Kaitlyn, a girl Joey had had a crush on for several months now.

"What you did in there was really dumb," Travis said.

"Dumb? Treating my friends to pizza is dumb? Who're you to say?"

"Just tell me how much money you budget each payday for eating out? Whatever it is, you probably blew it for the whole month."

"Budget, smudget. I don't need a budget. This is summer and a budget is like doing math. You know how much I hate math."

Travis stopped talking then, because he knew he was taking

IT'S A TEEN'S LIFE

the wrong approach with his cousin. He should have known better and kept his mouth shut in the first place.

A few days later, he called Joey asking him to go with him to the coffee shop. "I have someone I'd like you to meet," Travis told him.

Joey agreed and when they arrived at the coffee shop, there sitting in their favorite booth was Craig and another guy about Craig's age.

At the sight of Craig, Joey rolled his eyes and heaved a sigh. Turning to Travis, he said, "I don't know what you've got up your sleeve, but I should have known Craig would be involved."

"Just hold on. This isn't about Craig—he just happens to know this guy I want you to meet. You've been talking about being an entrepreneur. Well, you're gonna meet a real live entrepreneur. A very young one."

As they approached the booth, Craig made introductions all round. The guy with him was Terrance Hanley.

"Wow. I've heard of you," Joey said, as he skootched in beside Terrance. "You're the kid who started the news digest app program and then sold it to some gargantuan company for big bucks."

"That would be me," Terrance replied with a big smile.

Craig moved over and waved for Travis to sit beside him.

"So, Craig," Joey said, "how would a guy like you know a superstar like Terrance?"

Craig laughed. "I happen to be in an entrepreneurial group that several of us started at the university. We asked Terrance to come in and host one of our mastermind sessions."

Joey looked at Travis and silently mouthed, *entrepreneurial group?* Travis could tell Joey was little overwhelmed at this bit of news.

After they'd all ordered their favorite coffees and Danish, Terrance said, "So Joey, I hear you hold some entrepreneurial aspirations. What would you like to know? I'm open. Ask away."

Travis could tell by the look on Joey's face that he was in heaven. For almost forty-five minutes he lobbed questions, and Terrance had wise and insightful answers for each one.

At one point, the subject turned to the skill of handling money. "How you handle the small amount of money you have in your possession today," Terrance said, "will directly affect how you will handle large amounts of money on down the road.

"I've seen entrepreneurs start out with great ideas and substantial backing," he went on, "but due to their failure to handle their cash wisely, they crashed and burned. And it's not pretty."

"But what if you hate math?" Joey asked. "Which I do."

"What if you hated to brush your teeth? Or take a shower?" Terrance countered. "You just do what needs to be done. I bet there are some things your mom doesn't really enjoy doing, but she gets the job done, right? So you have clean clothes to wear and dinner is on the table. Managing money is something you do whether you like it or not."

Joey nodded, but Travis could tell he was uncomfortable with the turn in the conversation.

"When I first started out," Terrance explained, "I had to know to the exact penny how much was coming in and how much was going out."

"Kinda like a budget?" Joey asked.

Terrance laughed. "Like a budget on steroids!"

At that, Joey glanced over at Travis and gave his famous sheepish grin.

Terrance turned serious for a minute. "It's a sure sign of maturity, Joey, when you take responsibility for budgeting your income and expenditures. Find a system that works for you, then use it."

"System?"

"Yeah, like a budgeting app. Run an online search and find the one that works best for you. They're super simple to navigate."

"Never thought of that," Joey admitted. "That wouldn't seem so much like math class, would it?"

"Nope," Terrance answered. "It'd be more like playing a video game where you always win."

Joey laughed. "Always win. I like that."

· · · · ● ● · · · ·

Why Create a Budget

Joey learned a lot from Terrance who, he later discovered, was a millionaire several times over. Mainly he learned that he didn't have to necessarily *enjoy* budgeting. He just had to step up, take control, and *do it*.

When you're young, your income is likely limited; you do all in your power to stretch every dollar. One tool that can assist you with that is a well-thought-out budget. A budget is basically a roadmap of your financial life. It allows you to plan your expenses so you don't spend more money than you have coming in.

Without a budget, you'll be tempted to spend money on things you don't need. If you spend recklessly on the very day you get your paycheck, you'll soon find that you run out of money before that pay period is over. That means you're scrounging for a few bucks to last you till next payday.

Now you're stuck, and may be tempted to charge items on your credit card (if you have one) to cover your outstanding expenses. Then, because you fail to budget the next month, you won't have the money to pay the balance on the card. Interest will start piling up, and you can easily find yourself caught in the awful pit known as *debt*.

Once you set up a budget and learn to live by it, you will be more in control over the feeling of chaos you may have about your finances. If your goal is to stay out of debt, it will involve making difficult choices; you can't have it all. Creating a budget allows you to make informed, purposeful decisions as to how to allocate your money in the best way to reach your goals.

How to Create a Budget on Paper

Creating a budget on paper is pretty simple, but maintaining it can be difficult. It requires discipline. I recommend the online service Mint (https://www.mint.com) for creating and sticking with a budget, because most teens are online most of the time anyway.

Of course there is always the pen-and-paper option because:

1. Some folks like doing things by hand.

2. Going through the steps on how to create an offline budget is a good way of learning the basic principles, regardless of format.

3. Even if you don't plan on doing a budget on paper indefinitely, you might want to try it a few times in order to reinforce those principles.

Assess Your Monthly Income

Gather your pay stubs and figure out exactly how much you take home each month (or each pay period). If you're self-employed or do work on the side, make a close estimate of how much you earn a month. You need to know how much money you have to work with before you start creating your budget. You can't figure out what to spend, if you aren't sure how much you make.

List Fixed Expenses

Fixed expenses are those items that stay roughly the same each month. They include things like rent, car insurance, car payments, health insurance, phone bill, and student loan payments. For teens like Travis and Joey, they won't have many bills to pay. However, their parents may require them to put gas in the car when they use it, or to buy their own clothes, etc. And be sure to figure in the amount you want to save out of each paycheck.

Subtract Total Fixed Expenses from Total Monthly Income

The amount that's left over after fixed expenses is what you have to spend on variable expenses. If your fixed expenses are more than your total monthly income, you're in trouble, as you haven't even gotten to your variable expenses yet.

Time to do a close check on expenditures–where can spending be cut? If you're already living away from home, this item may include cutting back on the cable bill, downgrading your cell phone plan, getting a roommate to reduce rent costs, and so on.

Set Spending Goals for Variable Expenses.

Once you know how much money you have to work with, budget for variable expenses. These are the expenses that fluctuate from month-to-month. Unlike fixed expenses, variable expenses can be something you can more easily control to some degree. These are the areas where you can cut back the most and start getting ahead in your finances. This might include eating out, phone apps, movies, entertainment, and the latest technology gadget. Set a reasonable spending goal for each variable expense. Having a budget allows you to clearly see where you might be overspending.

Subtract Total Expenses (Fixed and Variable) From Monthly Income

The goal, obviously, is for you to spend less than you earn. If you're spending more than you earn, it's time to tweak expenses and cut back. Look at your budget to see where you may be spending money on things you don't really need. As in the case of Joey buying pizza for his friends when, in all reality, he couldn't afford to do so.

If, after all the calculating, you see that there is a surplus—set up a savings account and deposit it there. As mentioned in the previous chapter, out of sight, out of mind. Money you don't see, is money you usually will not spend. In a few months, or a year, you'll look at that savings account and feel quite proud of yourself for the amount you've saved up.

Keep Track of Spending

After you've created the budget for the month, keep track of every single penny you spend to ensure that you stay within your budget. (Can't you just hear Joey exclaiming, "Every *single penny*?")

If this sounds extreme, let's take a closer look. If fifteen random teens were asked how much money they spent a month on, say, soft drinks, snacks at the convenience store, and their favorite cappuccinos at the coffee shop, chances are none would have the correct amount. Most would guess way below what they actually spend. This is just one small example of how money can drain right out of your pocket, week after week, month after month. For you it might be online video games–you just *have* to have the latest version. Whatever it is, find the *money leaks,* and begin to get them under control.

Many people who begin this discipline (even adults) are quite surprised to discover where their money leaks are.

Get in the habit of grabbing every receipt—at the coffee shop, at the convenience store, at the movie theater. Tuck those receipts into your wallet or purse. This will be a big help when you go to tally up the month's spending.

Keeping track of every expenditure will also help when you make next month's budget. As you review how much you spent the previous month, you can adjust your spending accordingly. Keeping track of expenditures is probably the hardest part of budgeting, and where most people fail. It takes practice to get in the habit. The best part is that learning this while you're young will benefit you for many years to come.

Review Your Budget Every Month

Each month, go over last month's budget to see how you did. You'll be able to see where you did well and where you can improve. After you review, repeat the whole process and make next month's budget.

Time to Automate

For years, I kept my budget on paper, but eventually I switched over to the online system, Mint (https://www.mint.

com/). I would never go back to writing it all out on paper. In my opinion, this is the only way to go.

Mint's free online service takes all the hassle out of tracking your spending. When you sign up for Mint, you'll be asked to connect all your financial accounts (checking, credit cards, loans, etc.) into their system. Don't worry. Mint uses the same 128-bit encryption and physical security that banks use. Their practices are monitored and verified by TRUSTe, VeriSign, and Hackersafe, and are supported by RSA Security. And besides, Mint is a "read only" platform. So if someone does hack into your account, they wouldn't be able to move money out of it.

Track Spending Automatically

Once you have your financial accounts connected to Mint, just use your debit card as you normally would. Mint automatically tracks and categorizes your spending for you. So, for example, if you pick up groceries at the super-market, Mint will automatically categorize the purchase as "groceries." It's almost magical how good Mint is at catego-rizing things automatically.

	MAY 15	Whole Foods	Groceries		-$56.09
☐	MAY 15	Starbucks	Coffee Shops		-$3.27
■	MAY 15	Amazon	Shopping	▼	-$41.99

DETAILS Appears on your ABC Bank statement as **AMAZON.COM** AMZN.COM08/28C on May 15   SPLIT

TAGS ☐ Reimbursable ☐ Spouse

Manage your tags

Cancel   I'm Done

The system is flexible; if you don't like the way it categorizes your spending, you can change it, and Mint will start organizing those transactions the way you prefer. There are times when the system gets things wrong or doesn't know how to categorize a transaction, but correcting it isn't difficult. Once the correction is made, Mint gets right back on track.

Tweak Mint's Suggested Budget

After a few weeks of tracking your income and spending, Mint will create charts and graphs that are easy to understand and show you exactly where your money is going. Using this information, Mint will create a suggested budget for you that you can then tweak to meet your financial goals.

What's great about this tool is that as you adjust your budget, Mint will show you charts in real time, letting you see how those changes will affect the amount of money you'll have left over at the end of the month.

Let Mint Remind You If You're Getting Off Track

Mint will send warnings to your email or cell phone when it notices that your current spending habits have put you on a trajectory that will overshoot your allocated budget. They'll also send you alerts when certain bills are due.

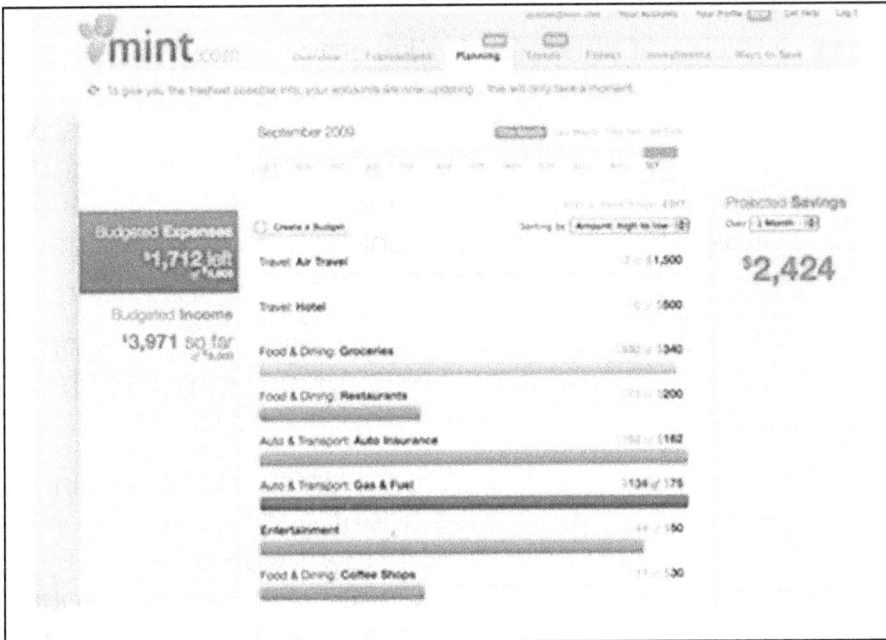

Review and Adjust as Needed

I log into Mint every week to see how things are going with my spending and budgeting. Mint's easy-to-read charts make reviewing a breeze. If I need to clamp down on my budget, I make the adjustment and Mint takes care of the rest.

The 50/30/20 Budget Rule of Thumb

As you sit down and put pen to paper (or fingers to your keyboard), to figure out your budget, you may find yourself getting overwhelmed. There can be so many numbers and details, you may wonder if your budget is actually realistic. It's helpful to have a benchmark or rule-of-thumb to compare your budget to see if you're on the right track.

One rule of thumb that you might find helpful was coined by Harvard bankruptcy law professor, Elizabeth Warren. It's called the 50/30/20 Budget Plan and calls for the following:

- Limit 50% of your after-tax income to *needs* like rent, utilities, food, health insurance, and car insurance. You need to be strict about what you classify as a *need*. A cell phone plan with unlimited data and texting isn't a need; cable isn't a need; grass-fed buffalo steaks or Super Sonic burgers, while they may be food, aren't needs either.

- Limit 30% percent of your after-tax income to *wants*. Clothes, eating out, cell phone plans, movies, subscriptions to magazines, apps, and so on.

- Spend at least 20% of income on savings or paying down debt. If you have student loans or credit card debt, work on paying that down with at least 20% of your monthly income. Once you pay down your debt, shift to putting that money into retirement savings.

Again, this is just a rule of thumb to offer some guidance. You can adjust it if you want to be more aggressive with your debt repayment or savings. But if your spending roughly matches the 50/30/20 breakdown, you can be confident that you're on the right track financially.

(This material was based on information from this site: www.artofmanliness.com/2012/08/16/how-to-create-a-budget)

How to Control Spending

Before we close out this chapter on budgets and budgeting, let's take a look at a few strategies to help you to control your spending.

- Don't carry around a wad of cash. Having too much money in your wallet will always make you feel like you have more to spend than you really do.

- Beware of the dangers of debit and credit cards. Both act as *invisible spending machines.* The debit card takes money directly out of your checking account. Rack up too many purchases and your account will be overdrawn. More about credit cards and debt in a later chapter–suffice to say at this point, avoid using them for *easy money.*

- Split the restaurant bills fairly between friends and family

- Be wary of lending money to a friend. They may promise to pay you back, but will they?

- With every purchase of more than $10 or $20, stop and ask yourself, "Do I really *need* this? Or is it just a whim?"

- Set up a plan to put a certain amount in your savings account each month. This will be your "off limits" money.

- Instigate a trading session with friends. Does someone have something you want; and you have something of equal value that they might want? As has been said, "One man's junk is another man's treasure." This could save a lot of money.

- Or instead of trading, set up an account on eBay, and post and sell what you can live without.

Get creative with money. It's not always about spend, spend, spend. You're smarter than that!

In the next chapter we're going to tackle a very interesting subject–taxes!

CHAPTER 7

THE BAD NEWS: TAXES

Travis and Joey paid for their snacks and soft drinks at the corner convenience store and as they pushed through the doors and headed for the car, Travis said, "Thank you, Mr. Citizen, for paying your taxes."

"Huh? What's that supposed to mean?"

"You were bellyaching the other day about all the money that was being taken out of your paycheck for taxes. I was giving you a reminder that you just paid taxes. You can't get away from taxes."

They piled into Travis's dad's car. It was one of those rare summer evenings when they were both off work. They were headed to the pool for a swim.

"Yea for Trav–I can always count on you to bring up good news. So what taxes did I just pay, oh older, wiser cousin?"

"Sales tax. Our state and our city charges sales tax. Look at your receipt."

Joey pulled the wadded receipt out of his pocket. He'd been faithfully training himself to hang on to receipts to keep track of his spending. "I spent $7.68."

"And how much tax?"

"Hm. Sixty-eight cents."

Travis put his drink in the holder and started the car. "Okay, let's do a little more math. Oh, sorry, I know you hate math."

"True. But I want to know where you're going with this."

"We'll round up the $.68 to $.70. And just for grins and giggles, let's say you made this same purchase every day for a year. What does that add up to?"

Joey pulled out his phone and brought up his calculator app. "Three hundred sixty-five times $.70. Wow. Trav, that comes to $255.50! Who'd have guessed?" Joey unwrapped his sandwich and started chowing down. "So what's your point?"

"My point is we've been paying taxes nearly every day of our lives. Now that we both have jobs, we're paying another kind of tax. Our parents have to pay property taxes on the houses we live in. That's yet another kind of tax. And when they buy license plates for the car, that's a type of tax. And the list goes on." He handed his sandwich to Joey. "Here, unwrap this for me."

Joey unwrapped the sandwich and handed it back to Travis. "Sheesh. I never gave taxes much thought before, but they're everywhere."

"Something we gotta live with now that we're almost adults. You've heard that old saying, *There's only two sure things in life – death and taxes.*"

Joey nodded. Then around a mouthful of sandwich added,

"And don't forget a Monday morning pop quiz in Coach Wallace's history class. That's a sure thing."

"You've got a point there, Joey," Trav replied.

. . . . . ● . . . . .

The Bridge to Independence

The teen years are like a bridge, moving a person from childhood and transitioning over into adulthood. Little by little, more independence is being experienced, as well as new things to learn about. Like taxes.

In Chapter 4, we listed the amounts that an employer withholds from the employee's paycheck and the reason for each one. In this chapter, we'll go a bit deeper into the subject of taxes. That ever-certain thing that Travis talked about.

Will You File a Return Separate from Your Parents?

The criteria for your filing a return on your own is based on three factors:

1. Are you considered a dependent by the IRS?

2. How much income did you make?

3. What type of income did you earn?

You are a dependent if:

- You are under 19

- If you're under 24 and you're a full-time student

- If you live in your parents' home more than 50% of the year

- If you do not provide more than half your own financial support

From here it becomes a little more complex because the IRS looks at different types of income.

Unearned Income

Unearned income is income generated from dividends, interest or investment gains—or a combination of both.

Earned Income

If you are a dependent who has no unearned income, you will file a separate tax return if the earned income is above the standard deduction. ($6,300 for 2015). So if you earned less than that, you would not *have* to file.

However, it's a good idea to file anyway. If your employer withheld federal income tax, there may be a refund coming to you at the end of the year. That's your money, and you don't want to pass it up. Also, just the act of filing your own return is a great learning experience.

Information Needed to File Your Annual Tax Return

Besides basic information about yourself (name, address, date of birth, etc.), you'll receive tax forms in the mail from your employer and any banks you do business with. The most common of these forms are:

- A W-2 from your job that reports the salary, wages, and tips you made. Your employer must mail your W-2 to you by February 1st each year. Many employers offer electronic versions via the same website where you can view your paycheck stubs. If you worked more than one job during the year, you'll receive a W-2 for each one.

- If you received any unemployment income, you'll get a 1099-G from the state that paid you.

- If you made $10 or more in interest from a checking or savings account, your bank will send you Form 1099-INT, otherwise you can use online banking or your account statements to determine the interest you made.

There are less common forms you may receive as well. They'll be mailed by early February at the latest.

Preparing Your Tax Return

When it comes down to actually preparing the tax return, you have several options:

Getting Help from Parents

Most teenagers will no doubt turn to their parents for assistance in this task. Parents have been dealing with the IRS for many years. They either do all their taxes themselves, or they have a computer program to help, or they have an accountant who does all the grunt work.

Pen and Paper

The old-school way to do your taxes is with pen and paper. It takes a while and some tax knowledge, but you can't beat the price. Determine the forms and schedules you need, download them from the IRS, print them, and get cranking. Once you're done, mail your completed return to the IRS along with your W-2 and a check (if you owe additional taxes). This is a great way to learn the basics.

Pay Someone Else

There are so many tax services in existence today, from the local "tax store" to quick and easy online programs. And then, of course, there are accountants and CPAs who will prepare tax returns for a fee. Their services are not cheap. Prices may start at around $100, and can run up to $200 or $300 or more–especially if you happen to have complicated finances. They send your return and the needed paperwork to Uncle Sam for you.

I prefer this option as you reduce the chances of mistakes and have confidence that you are in compliance with the current tax laws. But you may want to save using that service until you are older.

Do It Yourself with Your Phone or Computer

As mentioned, online tax software has revolutionized the tax preparation industry. This software uses an interview format–it asks a series of questions and then creates the correct tax forms based on the answers given.

The program does all the math for you, puts the numbers in the right places, and checks for mistakes. This ensures that you get the biggest refund possible. Once you're done, your return is filed electronically with IRS e-file.

Personally I like TaxAct (https://www.taxact.com). I feel it's one of the better programs out there. You can try it for free and don't pay until you're happy with the program.

Looking for My Refund

Most taxpayers get a refund, which is very welcome at any time, and especially as the new year starts. The amount of the refund will depend on your income and how much was withheld from your pay. When you file your return, you are given the choice to have the IRS send a check or make a direct deposit into your bank account. Direct deposit is significantly faster, so obviously, that's the best. Plus, when it is placed into your account without passing through your hands, you're much less likely to spend it.

In a rare case if you owe taxes (seldom, if ever, do teens owe on their income tax), you simply write a check and enclose it when you file your return. Or you can extend permission for the IRS to withdraw the money from your bank account electronically.

How You View Paying Taxes

There a balance to how you view filing taxes returns—on the one hand, they should be taken seriously; however, they're not something to be dreaded, or put off. As you can see from the information in this chapter, it's quite a simple process.

Be sure you keep copies of every filing. If you make a major purchase in the future, a loan department usually asks to see three years of tax returns. This is especially true when buying a home. While that may be down the road, it's still important to get in the habit of keeping copies of all important documents–and that includes tax returns.

Well, what do you know about this? We're going from one negative subject to another—from taxes to debt. They may not be the most pleasant subjects, but both are certainly important to understand.

CHAPTER 8

CAUTION: BAD DEBT CAN RUIN YOUR LIFE

It was noisy in the pizza place which was filled with kids from their school. Travis noticed that Joey seemed to have learned his lesson about picking up the tab just to make a showing. He didn't offer to pay for anyone's bill but his own.

The two cousins were across the table from one another, when halfway through the evening, their friend, Conner, pulled out his wallet.

"Hey, you guys, you'll never guess what I got." Opening his wallet, Conner pulled out a brightly-colored credit card sporting the logo of his favorite NFL team.

The response was probably exactly what Conner was looking for. Oohs and ahhs sounded from all around the table, and remarks like, "Way to go man," and "So cool."

Travis looked across the table at Joey and saw that his cousin was duly impressed. His eyes were wide.

"I've been reading up on how important it is to establish good credit while you're young," Conner explained to his attentive audience. "So I'm starting right now."

Conner was one of the older seniors in the group having had to repeat a class when he was still in grade school. At eighteen, he was able to get a credit card on his own.

Sarah, the brainiac of their group, wasn't joining in the praise. "Welcome to the first step into the bottomless pit, Conner."

Sarah was sitting right beside Joey, and at her comment, his head whipped around to face her. "So what's that supposed to mean, Sarah?" Joey went to defensive mode. "It's pretty obvious that Conner's done his research on this."

Conner was nodding. "Joey's right. I've learned how important it is to develop a good credit record, and having a credit card is a good way to do it."

"Like one chance in a thousand *that's* going to happen," Sarah said. "Did you look through all the papers that came with your card? Did you see the one in there that said, 'Enclosed herein is your guaranteed setup for failure'?"

"Ouch. That's getting pretty rough," Conner said. "I don't know what you're talking about."

"That's okay," Sarah told him," you're about to find out."

When the little gathering broke up, Travis grabbed Joey's arm and dragged him over to where they could talk to Sarah out of earshot of the others.

"Sarah," Travis said, "I want to know the reasons behind what you were saying. You sound like you know what you're talking about."

Sarah looked at Travis for a moment to be sure he wasn't making fun of her. Then she said, "Tell you what, let's do this. Are you off work tomorrow?"

"I am."

"I'll meet you at the library at two, and I'll show you exactly what I mean."

"Joey wants to come too."

Joey wasn't so sure. "I've got some other things going on…"

"But nothing that can't be put off, right Joey? I'll come by and get you."

Travis had for a long time wanted to get to know Sarah better, and this seemed the perfect setup.

Joey said, "Okay, we'll be there. But can you make it short?"

Sarah smiled sweetly. "Oh it'll be short – and quite to the point."

When the cousins arrived at the library the next afternoon, they expected to see Sarah right there waiting for them. She was not.

"I think we've been stood up," Joey said, sounding relieved. "Let's go."

"Not so fast. We haven't even looked around."

After scouring the place, they finally found Sarah upstairs sitting at a table near where all the books on money and finance were stored.

"Oh cute," Joey muttered under his breath.

"Be nice," Travis warned him.

"I'm trying."

The boys pulled up chairs across from Sarah. She didn't even say hi, but pointed to a pile of papers in front of her. "These are the types of papers that a person receives when a card is issued to them. But let's step back a minute. I'll begin by identifying exactly what a credit card is. It gives you a way to spend money you don't have. Pure and simple."

She was rummaging through the papers. "It's money you'll have to pay back sooner or later, and usually you'll be paying back more than you spent, due to interest and fees." Looking at Joey, she asked, "Would you have any idea the APR on Conner's new card?"

Joey looked confused. "The what?"

"APR. Annual percentage rate."

"Oh, you mean the interest rate," Joey said. "I heard him say that there's no interest. Zero. Zilch. That why he knew it was the card he wanted. He knew it was a good deal."

"Do you have any idea what might cancel out that zero APR?"

"I don't think anything would," Joey replied.

Travis had an idea, but he kept quiet. Joey seemed to really be getting into this conversation.

"That's where you're wrong," Sarah said. She proceeded to show Joey in the *guide*–which was in the tiniest print Travis had ever seen–where it said that if a payment was ever late, the normal interest rate would apply. "Do you know what that *normal* interest rate might be?"

Joey shook his head.

"Says here that it's 18.9%. That's a hefty fee for using a card to buy things that you have no money to buy in the first place. In other words, you don't have enough money to pay for what you want, so you spend more money to pay for it with a credit card. How does that make sense?"

Joey was shaking his head. "But," he protested, "Conner has a great job. I'm sure he'll never make a late payment."

"Maybe. I hope so. But just for your future reference, if you make an online payment one minute after midnight on the due date, it's late. Always remember—expect the best, plan for the worst," Sarah said.

"Huh?"

"I think she means there could come up an emergency and you just might be late on a payment," Travis put in.

"Travis is right. Do you know that amount of the late fees for most credit cards?"

Joey shook his head.

Again Sarah found it in the guide and pointed to it.

"Up to $35," Joey read.

"So," Sarah said slowly, "let's say you spent $50 on a nice pair of neon Nikes. They're on sale, and because they're on sale, you feel you can't pass up this great savings. You put it on your credit card because you're short on cash. But also because you're short on cash, you don't make your card payment on time and they charge you $35. Plus, now–because you've lost your zero APR–they're charging interest on that $50 item that was on sale."

Sarah was quiet for a moment and let her words soak in. Then she added, "You tell me, Joey. How is that a good deal?"

Joey just shrugged. Travis could tell Sarah was hitting home.

"This is how millions of Americans get trapped. Credit card companies care nothing about you—or your credit, which Conner mentioned yesterday. They're in business to make money, and they make money due the ignorance of people who want to spend money they don't have. And they start young, with teens like us. Like Conner."

Joey slouched a little lower in his chair. "How do you know about all this anyway? How can you see what Conner and the others don't see?"

Sarah gathered up the papers, stacked them neatly, folded them, and stuck them in her purse. "My father's a financial planner. He's been drumming this into my head since I was in first grade."

"Sheesh," Joey said, shaking his head. Just then he brightened. "Hey, I got an idea. Let's start an after-school club where we talk about stuff like this. To help other teens not get trapped."

Sarah stood to her feet and smiled at Joey. "I already have. Started it at the beginning of the school year last fall."

"Really? What's it called?" Joey wanted to know.

"Financial Literacy 101."

Travis leaned over to Joey. "You probably wouldn't have been looking for a club with that name."

"Guess not."

"See you guys," Sarah turned to leave.

"Yeah, see you." Joey replied, still in a fog. "And thanks, Sarah."

"Anytime."

Travis was already trying to figure out a way that he could connect with Sarah again at some future date.

. . . . . ● . . . . .

To Conner, his new credit card was like a bright shiny promise of his ability to buy nice things. Having it in his wallet made him feel like he had it altogether. Joey was wishing he could experience that same feeling. However, after listening to Sarah, he had a different perspective.

Live Within Your Means

It's never a matter of how much money you have, it's all about *what you do with the money you have*. The reason so many people get caught in the debt trap is because they fail to use a budget to live within their means. (Budgets were discussed in Chapter 6.) People often desire immediate gratification by buying what they want, instead of planning and saving for what they truly need.

People start working, get promotions, make more money, but still live paycheck-to-paycheck because their expenses increase right along with their income. To them, more money means a nicer car, a bigger house, eating out more often at better restaurants, more vacations, designer clothes. The list goes on and on.

It's easy to rationalize your situation and then justify expenses, chalking it up to improving a perceived quality of life. Let's take a new car, for instance. The truth is, a car is a vehicle to get you from point A to point B; the brand of car, or how much it costs, is irrelevant.

The sad fact is, as our income increases, seldom does our savings account increase; seldom does our retirement account increase. And all because of a lack of responsible spending habits.

Most American families are one paycheck away from financial disaster, because they have nothing saved. You don't have to be that person. Decide now that you will be financially independent. This will bring you a feeling of power, satisfaction, and control in your life. Here are a few ways that people get into trouble with debt.

Credit Cards

10 Facts Teens Should Know About Credit Cards

1. **A credit card is a contract.** When you sign up for a credit card, you agree to certain terms and conditions. When you buy something, you have already agreed that you will pay them for every dollar you spend.

2. **Unpaid bills put you further and further behind.** They lower your FICO score, which is a score that may be important to your financial future. In your teenage years, you should be getting ahead financially, not falling behind.

3. **A credit card offer in the mail does not make you special or important.** Owning a credit card does not make you cool. I remember the teen years – everything is about status. Somehow our teens are being taught that a credit card is a status of adulthood.

4. **The minimum payment is not what you should pay – pay the balance in full.** It really sounds like the credit card company is cutting you a deal. "You owe me $150, but I'll just take $25 for now." Never pay the only minimums. Pay your balance in full every month.

5. **"Grace period is not an act of kindness."** This is another deceptive term. Once again, they make it sound like

the credit card company wants to buddy up. I've found that if I don't pay the bill right away, I'm more likely to forget to pay the bill. As a result, I pay the balance when I get the bill.

6. **Get the right credit card for you.** The best way to get a credit card is to **match your needs with credit card features**. This typically does not come in the form of a direct mailing. If you want a credit card, shop around and find the card that has the best features for your needs, not the logo of your favorite sports team. For example, locate a 0% APR credit card, a 0% balance transfer, or rewards credit card.

7. **A higher credit limit is not the goal.** In many ways, a high credit limit can be dangerous. Instead, decide how much you might need and ask the credit card company to lower your limit to that amount. Typically, a teen's limit does not need to be above $500.

8. **Interest rates and fees.** Credit card companies make their money by charging interest and fees. The more interest you pay, the less money you have to save towards your future. Believe me, your future self won't be too happy if all he or she can do is pay interest.

9. **Never lend your credit card or credit card number.** Also, credit card companies will never ask for your account information. If someone calls and asks for your credit card information, hang up the phone and dial the 1-800 number on the back of the credit card.

10. **People spend more money with credit cards than cash.** I've tracked my own spending, and I agree that people do spend more with credit than cash. So why do people keep using credit cards? Basically, because credit cards have advantages over cash.

http://cashmoneylife.com/credit-card-tipsfor-teens/

The Bottomless Pit

Credit cards are how people get themselves into bad debt. They spend money they don't have, make minimum payments, and accumulate a mass of interest and debt until they exceed their income to pay it off. This is the bottomless pit that Sarah was referring to.

Credit cards can be very dangerous—it's much better if you simply use your checking account debit card. That is the safest way to go. If you don't have the money, don't make the purchase. (A debit card works by drawing money out of your checking account immediately when you make your purchase.)

If you do get a credit card, limit yourself to one or two for emergency situations and to help you build your credit history. When you have to use them, always make sure you have enough money in your checking or savings account to cover the purchase. When the bill comes due–pay the full amount every time. No exceptions!

Check This Out

When a credit card holder runs up a large debt amount, it becomes overwhelming, and they begin paying only the minimum payment amount. All the while, the interest on this debt is growing and growing. If this continues, eventually the interest amount could exceed the original purchase.

Here's a graphic example. Let's say you have charged $2,000 on a credit card in one month and the interest rate is 18.5%. If only minimum payments are made and no new purchased were added to this card, it would take *eleven years* to pay off the debt. The amount of interest paid would amount to *$1,934*. This means that $2,000 purchase morphed into $3,934!

If every person who ever charged a purchase to a credit

card could grasp this concept, fewer people would ever get into credit card debt.

Store Cards

Almost every store you shop at will promote their store card. They offer you a discount on your purchase if you apply for a card with them that day. Don't do it! Just use cash or your debit card to make purchases at grocery, clothing, furniture and electronic-type stores.

There is a reason companies promote these cards–they can charge high interest rates and hope that you will make minimum balance payments when they send you bills each month, which many customers do. Companies make a lot of money off people when they accept store cards. They not only recoup the initial discount they gave you, but a lot more. Don't become a victim of this system. You don't need store cards in your wallet. Train yourself to always say, "No thank you."

Financing Purchases

You need a new computer from Best Buy, or new furniture from Rooms to Go. They will offer you incentives for applying for a store loan such as zero interest or no payment for the first year. It sounds *so* appealing. You tell yourself that you will put money aside over the next year so when the bill comes due, you will pay it all off.

If you are the type of person who can and will do that, fine. However, most people can't or don't. Then when the bills come (and they do), people get themselves into trouble. The interest that comes due creates a higher balance each month.

Only buy what you can afford at that time. If you don't have the money, save your money and then buy it when you have the amount saved up. Then–guess what? No interest cost to you. What a concept!

School Loans

I grew up in the UK where the perspective of education is somewhat different than in the United States. In the UK, most students, upon high school graduation, find training programs, or find jobs at companies that teach them a trade. In some cases, that company will pay them to go on to attend a university if it is needed to gain more theory.

I've lived in the US now for many years, and it still amazes me how many high school graduates attend a university, and choose degrees that they could just learn from an apprenticeship or intern program.

Choosing a Degree

I know many people who work in careers in which their degree has no relevance, which leads me to wonder–of what use was it to spend all those thousands of dollars on a college degree? Because a college education (especially these days) is extremely expensive, I strongly encourage you to choose your after-graduation plan wisely. If you do choose to get a degree, the best route is to obtain a specialty degree that will be required in your future chosen career.

Cutting Costs

One way of cutting back on expenses is to attend a community college for the first two years. This way you can complete all your college pre-requisite courses with a minimum of expense. These credits will transfer and will cost a lot less to obtain.

If you do go to college, make it your goal to successfully balance work, school, and recreation. Apply for as many scholarships as you can (one reason why getting good grades is so important), and earn as much as you can by working part-time. Many students approach college with the idea that student loans are a necessary part of getting a degree. This is not true. Try any way you can to reduce the amount of loans you will need.

A student loan is not free money. In fact, it is *very expensive* money. Student loans can haunt you for years to come. College graduates who enter the workforce saddled with a huge debt load from student loans are starting out with strikes already against them. For some, their payments are so large, they have little left to live on.

Think about this:

1. Seek every way possible to eliminate or reduce any loans for college

2. Beware of officials at your chosen school who try to "sell" you on their *best* loans. There have been instances where it was revealed that colleges were getting kickbacks from the very loan companies they were promoting. The best advice is to *do your research.*

3. There's no reason why college has to be completed in the "typical" four years. If it takes longer while you work to pay your way, you will be far better off.

In some instances, there is no way around taking on some debt to invest in your future—the key is to minimize the amount you will owe when you graduate. How much better it is to start off in your chosen career debt-free.

Major Purchases

When it comes to major purchases such as a car or a home, the situation is somewhat different than buying a couch or a new computer. Financing the purchase with a loan or mortgage may be your only option (it is for most people). Having a car and home to live in is essential. These are basic needs (transport and shelter), as opposed to *wants*.

But keep in mind, the type of home you live in and the car you drive does not define who you are as a person. Be responsible by ensuring you can comfortably pay the loan amount payments each month. A good rule of thumb is that your payments will not exceed 50% of your income, including your utilities and insurances.

Medical Bills

Healthcare in the United States is very costly. People without healthcare insurance can be only one unexpected hospitalization stay away from total financial disaster. They could end up with a huge bill that will require them to have a repayment plan for the rest of their lives. Do not think that because you are healthy, you won't have any health issues. You could get sick and diagnosed with some major chronic illness tomorrow, or be in a major car accident (which I personally experienced). Avoid this financial catastrophe by always having adequate healthcare insurance.

Gambling

Remember that Sarah described credit cards as a *bottomless pit*. Gambling can be described the exact same way. Gambling is more like lighting fire to your money and watching it burn away. The best advice is to *never* gamble away your hard-earned money.

Of course, there may be times you will go to Las Vegas, or a local casino, or a race track with friends just for fun. Never go to these places without a firm plan in place. Set a hard and fast rule that you will never bet what you can't afford to lose.

The safest way to have a fun gambling experience is to work out how much money you can afford to lose before you start. Next—stick to that budget. If you lose the money, then just know it was part of the experience.

If you win, great. But then, count yourself lucky and *walk away*. Remember that winning rarely happens, which explains why gambling establishments exist. Just like credit card companies, they are in business to make money, and they want to take yours!

It is very easy to fall into the trap that because you are winning, then bigger stakes won't hurt. Or if you are losing then you think that if you put a little more on this *certainty* you can get your money back. *Don't do it!*

Good Debt

As a final note, remember that it's a solid truth that you need to build a good credit history. Having a credit card, a car loan or a home mortgage—even though each one is a form of debt—they can be considered *good debt* if managed properly. Good debt helps you build your credit score. (More about credit scores in the next chapter.)

Just make sure you never take on too much expense, which then requires all your income just to pay these debts. You will be left with no money to set aside in savings, or to contribute toward your future retirement, or just to enjoy life. Also make sure you pay these debts in a timely manner each month. Pay the full required amount so interest does not accumulate which then transforms good debt into bad debt and defeats the whole purpose.

Remember when Conner stated that he planned to use his credit card to build good credit? Let's take a closer look at exactly what the term "good credit" actually means.

CHAPTER 9

MAKE PERFECT CREDIT A PERSONAL COMPETITION

Joey's dad made the best spaghetti in the whole county—or so Travis thought. And he loved it when his Uncle Rosano cooked up his signature sauce, simmered it almost an entire day, then the two families got together for a spaghetti feast.

On one such occasion, Joey and Trav were seated beside one another with their plates smothered with that famous spaghetti. They'd been too busy mowing back the food to pay much attention to the conversation flying around them. Their two sets of parents were noted for talking non-stop.

However, at one point when Craig started talking about possibly renting an apartment this fall, Trav listened up. He was thinking how neat it would be to have your own place.

"I thought it was a done deal," Craig was saying. "Brenden said he was all in and ready to go. We'd been talking for months about this plan. But come to find out, his credit score sucks, and we got turned down." Craig grabbed another piece of hot garlic bread from the platter in front of him. "He wants me to put the lease all in my name and him come in halves with me. But I don't like that idea."

Just then Trav's twelve-year-old sister, Allie, spoke up. "A credit score? What's a credit score? I never heard of a credit test. How did he get the failing score?"

Everyone at the table laughed which didn't set too well with Allie. Joey seemed to laugh harder than anyone else.

"What's so funny?" Allie demanded. "I just asked a simple question. What's credit anyway? Is it like a credit card?"

"You've asked a legitimate question," Craig told her, "and we're all laughing because having good credit, or bad credit as in Brenden's case, is about as confusing as you just stated."

Travis's dad, the accountant, chimed is. "It's like this, Allie. When a person uses a credit card, it's like borrowing money, and if they don't make their payments on time, it will reflect on their credit rating."

"I didn't know anyone could wreck their credit when they're as young as Brenden," Trav's mother chimed in. "That's horrible."

"Brenden charged up a bunch of credit cards last year, and it all got away from him," Craig explained. "And yeah, I agree, it is horrible."

Uncle Rosano said, "Seems to me such an irresponsible young man wouldn't be a good choice as a roommate, anyway. Maybe it's all for the best."

Allie was getting impatient with all this side talk. "But what's it mean about a score? And what's a credit rating? I still don't understand."

Joey, who had laughed the loudest, was no longer laughing. He leaned over to Trav and whispered, "I agree with Allie. I don't understand either. How does anyone know what your score is anyway?"

· · · · · ● · · · · ·

Credit

Who can blame Allie, or Joey either, for that matter? So much confusion reigns when it comes to credit ratings, credit scores, credit reports, and the list goes on and on.

In our present economy, having a good credit record is extremely important. A person's credit rating is often considered when:

- Applying for a school loan

- Purchasing a car

- Qualifying for a mortgage

- Acquiring a cell phone

- Leasing an apartment (as in the case of Craig and Brenden)

- And others…

When it comes to understanding personal finances, this component looms large. For some people, their opinion is that any kind of borrowing is to be avoided at all costs. For others, credit is an intoxicating license, an opportunity to reach for a lifestyle well beyond their means.

There can be a balance between these two extremes. Borrowing by using credit can be extremely helpful, or extremely harmful, depending on how it's used. It's best to view credit as a tool–a tool that will help you achieve a desired outcome.

Think of it like this: in the hands of an uneducated, unskilled, and inexperienced person, fire can cause havoc and harm. But in the hands of a responsible and educated individual, fire can be immensely useful. So it is with credit. For example, a bad use of credit would be buying a huge flat-screen TV with a credit card. Over time, as you are paying off your new TV, you are being charged interest each and every month. You are getting no *return* on this money spent. In fact, you are now paying *more* for the TV than you bought it for in the first place.

As was mentioned in the previous chapter, a good use of credit might be the purchase of a car that you need to transport you to and from your job. A car will put you in debt in the short-term, but will improve your financial prospects in the long-term.

Bottom line, there are wise ways in which to use credit, and there are not-so-wise ways in which to use credit.

What Is Credit?

Allie asked the simple basic question *What is credit?* Let's start there. The definition of credit is:

> *The ability to obtain goods or services before payment, based on the trust that payment will be made in the future.*

Student loans, car loans, home mortgages, and credit cards are all types of consumer credit instruments—you're getting money *now* to pay for something you otherwise couldn't afford. This is a loan that says the lender trusts you to pay them back at a later date.

As has already been mentioned, credit always comes with a price tag–and it's usually a high price tag. Banks, institutions, and stores, charge interest on the money they lend you. Basically, interest is the price you pay for the use of the funds, and the opportunity to pay that money back over an extended period of time.

Interest Rates

Different types of credit have different interest rates. Credit cards are notorious for having the highest interest rates among the various types of credit. This is because: 1) there's a higher risk that the credit card lender won't get repaid, and 2) it's more expensive to manage credit card debt (at least that's what the credit card companies say).

Creditworthy

Even among the same kinds of loans, you'll find different interest rates. That's because people have varying degrees of "creditworthiness." You'll often hear banks refer to people as having "good credit," "bad credit," or "no credit."

People with good credit have a reputation for being a responsible borrower. They pay their bills on time and manage the credit that's available to them responsibly. People with good credit not only have access to more money, they also get lower interest rates on their loans.

People with bad credit have a reputation for not paying their bills on time, or even not paying them at all. Banks and other businesses are less willing to extend credit to these individuals. Even if they're able to get a loan, a person with bad credit will be charged a higher interest rate.

Folks with no credit have no history of using credit, so they're kind of a wild card. They might be good with credit, or they might not. When banks loan money to people in this situation, they'll usually start off charging a higher interest rate, but they'll be willing to bring it down as the debtor proves they can, and will, faithfully repay the balance owed.

How Do Banks Know If You're Creditworthy?

So how do banks, or credit card companies, know whether you have good credit, bad credit, or no credit? When you apply for a loan, the person reviewing the application–in most cases–doesn't know you. That being the case, how could they know whether or not you can be trusted to pay them back?

The answer is that there are three big credit agencies keeping track of how you use credit—from how much you borrow, to how often you are late on payments. This goes on whether you know it or not, and it starts the minute you apply for your first credit card, or take on your first student loan.

Maybe you've seen commercials online and on TV about how to get your *free credit report*. (That's the record those Big Brother-like agencies have on you.) These commercials will also mention something called a *credit score*. Your credit score is the number that banks, and other lending institutions, use to determine whether or not you're a trustworthy borrower.

Many young people just getting their feet wet in the world of credit often confuse credit reports with credit scores, and vice versa. It's an easy mistake to make, but one that can be corrected with a quick primer on the difference between the two.

What's a Credit Report?

Credit reports explain what you *do* with your credit. They show when and where you applied for credit, from whom you borrowed the money, and to whom you still owe money.

Your credit report also tells if you've paid off a debt and if you make monthly payments on time.

Federal law mandates that all three major credit reporting agencies must each give you a free credit report each year. So, when those TV commercials talk about getting a free credit report, the above information is what they're offering.

A Word to the Wise

Getting your free credit report from a heavily-advertised site like www.FreeCreditReport.com or www.FreeCreditScore.com isn't a good idea. Here's the catch. Yes, you receive a free credit report and score, but you are then enrolled in their monthly credit-monitoring service for $15 a month.

You can get out of this if you cancel within seven days, but if you fail to do this, your subscription to their service will begin. This is wasted money. Making the cancellation is not a simple matter. You have to make a phone call rather than cancelling online. And you might forget (which is exactly what they're counting on).

Why fall for this trick when you can get your free credit report with no strings attached from www.AnnualCreditReport.com? This site offers a free report from each of the three credit agencies. You could order all three at once, but it's best to stagger them throughout the year. That way you can keep closer tabs on your credit score.

Why You Need to Request Your Credit Report Every Year

There are a couple of reasons why you should request a free credit report each year. First, it allows you to check for and correct mistakes that may have slipped into your report. When you spot a mistake, you can start taking actions to clean it up.

The second big reason you want to request a credit report every year is to protect yourself from identity theft. With the right information, a con artist can apply for credit cards in your name without you knowing it. Then you start getting calls from collection agencies asking you to pay up on purchases you never made. A yearly credit report lets you check to see if anybody is fraudulently using your name to apply for credit cards or loans without your knowledge and then you can take action if needed.

What's a Credit Score?

Remember Allie's remark at the dinner table:

"A credit score? What's a credit score? I never heard of a credit test. How did he get the failing score?"

Sometimes it feels like a test; and feels like we might be getting a *failing score.* But this is a little different.

Your credit score is determined by the information in your credit report. Credit scores are used by companies and banks to evaluate the potential risk posed by lending money to individual consumers. Your credit score determines if you qualify for a loan, what your loan's interest rate will be, and what your credit limit is. It's basically your trustworthiness score for lenders.

The company that came up with the idea of a credit score was the Fair Isaac Corporation. That's why you've probably heard credit scores referred to as a FICO score—an acronym for Fair Isaac Corporation.

Because each of the three credit agencies collect slightly different information, you could wind up with three different credit scores. Credit scores range from 500 to 850.

If you have a FICO score of 500, you're going to have a hard time getting a loan. Even if you manage to get one, the interest rate on it will be high. With any score above 720, you'll receive the best rates available.

Whenever you apply for a credit card or car loan, the banks and credit card companies use your credit score to determine whether to lend you money, or extend the credit card to you. Once you are approved, then they'll use your credit score to determine the interest rate that will be charged.

Ways in Which You Can Obtain Your Credit Score

- In recent years some credit card companies, and even a few auto loan companies, provide credit scores for customers on a monthly basis. The score may be listed on your monthly statement, or you can see it by logging in to your online account.

- If you have the need to seek credit counseling and use a non-profit counselor, they can often provide you with your report and your score. This is especially true with housing counselors approved by the U.S. Department of Housing and Urban Development (HUD). These counselors will also help you in reviewing your score and help you to understand what it all means.

- There are, as has been mentioned, many credit score services available. Some will advertise a "free credit score." Most are funded through advertising and therefore will not charge a fee. Still others will require you to sign up for a credit monitoring service with a monthly subscription fee in order to get your "free" score. Before you sign up for any of these services, be sure that you know what you are signing up for and how much it really costs.

- You can buy a copy your current FICO credit score

at myfico.com. Other services may also offer scores for purchase as well. If you decide to purchase a credit score, you are not required to purchase credit protection, identity theft monitoring, or other services that may be offered at the same time. Again, just be aware of what you're being asked to pay for.

How Your Credit Score is Determined

Because your credit score can possibly make or break some important financial and lifestyle decisions, it's important to understand how the credit agencies determine your score so you can take actions to ensure it's the best it can be.

When coming up with your FICO score, credit reporting companies look at several factors, including:

Payment Record

Your ability to pay your bills on time makes up 35% of your score. Payments that are more than 90 days late will hurt more than a payment that's just 30 days late. Also, recent late payments hurt more than older ones. A single late payment won't kill your score, so don't panic that you'll never be creditworthy because you missed a payment. Just pay the bill and try not to let it happen again.

Amount Borrowed Relative to Available Credit

This factor accounts for 30% of your score. The credit companies want to know if you're borrowing to the max. If you have $10,000 of available credit, and you consistently run a balance of $9,999, that's a red flag that says you're not very careful about your debt. However, if you have a balance of $200 of outstanding debt, that's a sign you're more responsible with credit. To improve your score, try to keep your debt to about 10% or less of your available credit.

Length of Credit History

This is 15% of your score. The longer you have successfully borrowed money and paid it back, the less risk you are to a lender. If you pay off a credit card, it's good to keep it open, even if you never use it. When you close it, you lose that credit history, which could, in turn, affect your score.

"Hard" Credit Pulls

A *pull* is a type of inquiry into your credit. This makes up 10% of your credit score. Hard credit inquiries are made by lenders for the purpose of extending you credit. These lower your score because they serve as a signal that you're looking for loans and are possibly a poor credit risk. This is why when the cashier at your favorite store asks if you want to sign up for a store credit card to get a discount, just say, "No thanks." This way you will avoid the hard credit pull.

If you're shopping around for a car loan or mortgage, lenders will have to pull your credit score every time you ask for a quote. Don't worry about those types of pulls hurting your score. Similar inquiries made within a two-week period won't ding your score.

Types of Debt

This is the final 10% of your score. It's best to have a mix of car, home, student loans, and little to no credit card debt. If you're up to your eyeballs in credit card debt, you'll be seen as bigger risk. (Those credit cards can be a monster!)

Other Factors

In addition to your FICO score, lenders will also take into

account other factors when determining whether to loan you money. Things like your income, job history, and any assets you own, can factor into whether you can secure a loan.

How Can I Build and Improve My Credit History and Score?

Because your payment record and length of credit history make up about 50% of your credit score, it's important for you to begin building a solid credit history as soon as you can. A good credit history along with a high credit score will serve you well later in life.

The fastest and surest way to build up your credit history is to simply open up credit accounts and pay back the money when it's due. Opening a credit card account is an easy way for young people to begin establishing their credit history. A low-interest, low-minimum-balance credit card can give a young person just starting out in life the opportunity to pay a credit balance on a regular basis in order to establish a solid positive payment record. Also, the earlier a young person obtains a credit card, the longer his credit history will be when he applies for that mortgage later in life.

There is a danger, though. This was discussed in Chapter 8. Credit cards can be a big-time hazard for teens just starting out on their own, because they allow you to spend money you don't have, as Sarah explained to Travis and Joey. "The bottomless pit," is how she described it.

The schedule of a young single person can be hectic and disorganized. Monthly payments can be overlooked, which leads to penalties and interest, and potentially plunging the card holder into further debt. If you don't have the income and level of responsibility to pay off the balance every single month, don't get a credit card. Just don't do it.

Even if you are responsible enough to get a credit card, maybe you don't like the idea. You prefer to avoid credit card debt altogether during your younger years. That's a smart move.

If, for whatever reason, you avoid getting a credit card, is there any other way to build up credit history? Or are you doomed to high interest rates when you apply for a mortgage later on in life?

If you're a college student, you may have student loans. As soon as you graduate, start paying your loans back on a consistent basis. This creates your credit history with no credit card.

Another method to create credit history without a credit card is to apply for a small loan through your local bank. Talk this over with your parents and have them co-sign on it. Set it up so you can make regular payments and pay it off as fast as you can. More credit history.

But let's say you've decided to not use credit at all: no credit cards, no student loans, no car loans. Nothing. Years into the future, when you're ready to buy a house, how will you be able to secure a low interest rate if you have no credit history?

PRBC Alternative Credit Score

PRBC stands for *Payment Reporting Builds Credit*. This is a relatively new concept that began in 2005 as a way to become financially credible without the use of credit cards.

Your PRBC Credit Score shows lenders you're financially responsible and trustworthy by keeping track of how well you pay non-credit bills like rent, utilities, and insurance on a regular basis. This alternative credit score is perfect for people who have:

- No credit
- Limited credit

- Poor credit

- Declined credit

The tide is turning and now there are many lenders who have come to accept a PRBC Alternative Credit Score when determining interest rates for mortgages and other loans. This is not like the credit reporting agencies that gather your information automatically. It's up to you to enroll online to create your own PRBC Alternative Credit Score. (https://www.prbc.com/)

In the next chapter, we'll talk about that famous first big investment for teens—buying a car!

CHAPTER 10

UBER IS NOT THE ANSWER: YOU NEED A CAR

Travis's dad referred to their Grandma Bess as the *Renaissance Woman*, but always in the kindest way. Only recently did Trav and Joey realize what that meant, but they knew it was true. Their Grandma Bess went everywhere, did everything, and had a wide variety of interests. She'd recently returned from a cruise, and the following week she was scheduled to run in a marathon.

But now she was in her kitchen serving up her famous, hot-from-the-oven, oatmeal-raisin cookies, which both boys loved. And both said their mothers (grandma Bess's two daughters), couldn't bake that same recipe and make cookies taste as scrumptious as Grandma Bess's. The boys sat at the kitchen table enjoying said cookies.

Trav's younger sister, Allie, was in the living room looking through old photo albums. She came in now, carrying one of the old albums. The photos which bored the boys, fascinated Allie.

"Hey, look at Grandma with her hair all backcombed, ratted, poufed, and sprayed," she announced, laying the album out on the kitchen table.

Grandma Bess rolled her eyes and laughed. "Thanks a lot, Allie."

"Hey," said Joey, looking at the other page, "get a load of the classic car."

Grandma Bess came over from the sink, leaned over and looked. "Sure wasn't a classic when we drove it," she said with a chuckle. "That's our old 1957 Ford Fairlane. Drove that thing for years. By the time we were done with it, it didn't look quite so classy."

Travis turned the album around so he could get a better look. "So why did you drive it for so long? Grandpa had a good job at the plant back then, didn't he? Couldn't you have traded it in for something better?"

Grandma Bess pulled out a chair and joined them at the table. "Now Travis, you remember your grandpa better than that. First of all, he scraped and saved to get this car, and bought it used from Dr. Langston. Paid the doctor in four or five payments and then it was his, free and clear."

"No car payments?"

"No car payments. While some of his other buddies were buying cars right off the showroom floor because of so-called *easy payments,* Charlie said he had better places to put his money than in a car. 'All I need,' he used to say, 'is something to get me from point A to point B, and a Ford can do it just as well as a Mercedes.'"

Joey laughed. "That sounds like Grandpa Charlie all right."

All the grandkids still missed their grandpa who had died a couple years earlier.

"He had that car when we got married, both your mamas came home from the hospital in that car, and both of them learned to drive with that car. And of course, he did most all the maintenance on it. We rarely had a mechanic's bill."

"Wow," was Joey's remark.

"So what *did* he spend his money on?" Travis wanted to know.

"Charlie talked a lot about depreciation. He preferred to invest in assets that would grow, not things that depreciated," Grandma Bess explained.

"Like his rental houses," Joey said.

"Exactly. And other investments. Which is why I don't have to look to your families to take care of me. Charlie made sure I'd always be taken care of financially." She looked at her grandchildren. "We weren't exactly thinking about grandkids when we made those financial decisions, but each one of you benefits today because of it."

"Wow." Joey's favorite word.

"I suggest you be thinking of your future grandchildren. And your future spouses, too. Do you want to bring a ton of debt into a marriage?" Grandma Bess stood up then and went back over to the sink. "What a bummer wedding present that'd be," she added.

On the way home, the boys had something new to think about. They'd both been looking online, and in the shopper papers, for possible cars to buy. Plus, browsing around used car lots.

"All I've been thinking about is just to get a car," Trav said. "Any car. To have something of my own to drive. Period."

"Yeah, me too."

"Maybe if I started saving more out of my paycheck, and if I spend time looking, and don't get in a hurry, I can find a reliable used car that wouldn't saddle me with a huge debt."

To Trav's surprise, Joey nodded his agreement. "I'd really like to be more like Grandpa Charlie," he said. "Because, when you think about it, buying a car is just the beginning. Then there's the insurance, gas, and all the upkeep. That's a humongous investment."

"I don't want to give my future wife debt for a wedding present."

"Fat chance," Allie piped up from the back seat. "No girl would even want to put up with you. Either one of you."

"Oh yeah?" Joey countered. "Wait'll some dude starts to even look in your direction–Trav and I are gonna chase him all the way into next week."

Allie groaned.

· · · · ● ● ● · · · ·

The Need for a Car

In the United States there are not many cities and towns that have sufficient public transportation. So if walking, riding a bike, or using public transportation doesn't suffice for your work/school life, sooner or later you will probably decide to buy a car.

If so, you will have to budget the amount that you can afford to pay out for a car payment, gas, maintenance, repairs, and insurance. Buying an older used car may your best choice. Research which makes and models have the best reputation for low maintenance and few needed repairs. You can easily find this information online. Or begin asking different people how reliable their car is.

Let friends and family members know you are in the market to make your car purchase. Sometimes someone knows someone who has a car they want to sell, but are not planning to use as a trade-in.

The Necessary Inspection

If you have one selected that you're serious about, take it in to a trusted mechanic, and ask them to do a thorough inspection from one end to the other. It may cost a few bucks, but is so worth it. They can see problems that you might never notice. If the seller will not allow you to take the car for a few hours to make that kind of inspection, then find another seller. They may be hiding something.

Ways of Financing

There are several ways you might make this purchase. If you know the seller, that person might be willing to set up a payment plan with you. A lawyer will be needed to draw up a contract.

Your parents may offer to make the purchase and you then make payments to them. This would be a little less formal, but it's still an agreement that you should make every effort to honor.

As another alternative, you might get a bank loan and have your parent co-sign, if they're willing. This would be a great way to begin to develop your credit standing.

Once the seller signs over the title to you, you are required to register the car at the Department of Motor Vehicles in your state.

Benefits of Leasing a Car

Another option might be to lease a car. Leasing is similar to financing the purchase of the car in many ways. You might be able to get more car for less money by leasing. A car loan is based on the full price of a new car, but a lease is based on only a percentage of the car's price.

Let's look at an example. On a $30,000 car, you'd finance the entire $30,000 purchase price with a car loan. With a car lease, you only pay the difference between the car's price and what it's expected to be worth at the end of the lease, which is a car's residual value.

If the car's residual value is 55% after three years, for example, that means the $30,000 car would be worth $16,500 at the end of the lease. You'd make lease payments on the remaining $13,500 and not the full $30,000.

The amount of your lease payments will depend on how large a down payment is made. You will see (or hear) advertised lease offers that tout their low payments, but the truth is that this is possible only with a large down payment. The down payment is negotiable; however, just keep in mind that if you put down as little as possible, you will have to expect those monthly payments to be higher.

You can expect a lease to be set up for three years, which is the length of many new-car warranties. The leasing company wants the car to be covered under warranty for repairs for the duration of the lease.

Your responsibility is general maintenance including oil changes, tire rotations, and other recommended maintenance from the manufacturer. If you fail to keep up your end of the contract, you could be facing extra fees when you turn the car in at the end of the lease.

As a teenager, you probably will not be considering leasing a car, but in the future, it may fit your needs perfectly. If you are the type of person who wants the newest high-tech features, leasing will be the way to go. A person who leases their cars never has to worry about selling the car or getting a good price for their trade-in. When the lease is up, the car is turned in and the customer walks away.

The Downside of Leasing

Mileage restrictions are often tacked onto a lease agreement. These restrictions can range from 9,000 to 15,00 miles a year. You will need to estimate how many miles you drive per year so you can determine how many miles to purchase. If you go over that amount, extra fees will be added at the end of the lease, and these overage charges can be very expensive.

With leasing, you can make minor alterations to the vehicle that can be reversed before you turn the car back in, but you can't make any major alterations. Read every line of the lease contract to be sure.

Leasing a car basically means that you're renting the car for a few years and paying interest to finance the rent agreement. Like renting a home, you're not building up any equity. If you ever choose to stop leasing that means a new car, with new payments, or you'll need to get a loan to buy the car you were leasing.

Keep in mind that only those with good credit are qualified to lease a car. If you have less-than-stellar credit, you will have to forego leasing, or wait until your score has been brought up to snuff.

Benefits of Buying a Car

Remember when Travis and Joey learned that their grandpa drove a car payment-free for many years? That's a strange concept for many families in this day and age. A car payment (or two) is as much a part of the budget as their mortgage payment.

When you purchase a car and pay off that loan, you now own that vehicle. It's yours. That monthly payment has disappeared from your budget. (What a happy day!) That's a great goal to strive for.

There is an element of pride in owning your own car, driving it until it's paid off, and longer, so you can enjoy a life of no payments. Then, in a few years, you can trade it in (if you so choose) and have the dealership buy it so you can use that money towards another car.

A person who is keeping a strict budget, and who pays off a car loan, will turn around, take that payment amount, and begin putting it in their savings.

Another benefit of buying a car is that there are no mileage restrictions. You can drive as much as you want with no worries of facing extra fees for going over a mileage limit.

Downside of Buying

When you buy a new car, you are not sure of its future resale value. Who knows what that vehicle will be worth when it's time to trade it in or sell it? When you lease, that future value is stated up front and added to the contract. If the car is worth less than that amount at the end, it's not your problem.

If you have a loan on a car and the car is worth less than what the loan is for, you have negative equity. This is known as being upside down on the loan. (More about an upside-down loan in the next chapter.) This means if you sell it or trade it in, you'll have to come up with the difference between what the car sells for, and the amount of money still left on the loan.

Another possible downside is that many lenders require about 10% to 20% down on a car loan. Let's say the price of the vehicle is $30,000. The down payment would be $3,000 to $6,000. That's a stretch for most people.

One other downside of buying is that in order to get the monthly payments to fit your budget, you may have to stretch out the length of the loan. Auto loans can last five years or more. Of course a longer loan means more interest paid out, which in the end makes the purchase more expensive.

(Remember when Grandpa Charlie said he had better things to spend his money on? This is why. A car payment can wreck a monthly budget in a hurry.) Always remember, the more you can pay up front, the lower the payment, the lower the interest, and the quicker comes the pay off!

No Such Thing as One-Size-Fits-All

When making the choice between buying or leasing your car, there is no such things as one-size-fits-all. It will all depend on your income, your budget, your needs, your credit rating, and on and on. Do research, ask lots of questions, then make the decision that works best for you. Avoid buying a vehicle only for how good it looks, or how good it makes you feel. This is a major purchase; it's a time to use wisdom.

Buying a newer car may mean the warranty is still in effect. However, an older, but still reliable, car may be a better purchase for someone with a smaller budget.

Be Wary of the Ads

Be wary of the advertisements and deals featured in your local newspaper. While dealerships are prohibited from false advertising, sometimes they will feature one vehicle for promotion. That one will sell out fast, which leave potential buyers showing up at the dealership to look at the more expensive inventory. If you see a deal that appeals to you, be sure to show up on the very first day of the promotion. Be the first one at the door and demand that they honor the advertisement. If they give any excuses, walk away.

A great way to do your research is through the website,

https://www.carmax.com. The site is easy to navigate and there are no salespersons to haggle with. Customers pay the full asking price every time, and the company prices the vehicles competitively.

Enter the car type, model, year of vehicle and search the country. Find the cheapest car available and use that price as your baseline for negotiation with other dealerships. Take a printout with you and show the dealership, then tell them this is the price you are willing to pay unless they can match or beat the price on a car they have in inventory. (The car which you actually like better than the one on carmax.com, but don't tell them that!)

In the event you discover the best price is actually on Carmax.com, then conduct one final step. Have Carmax.com provide you with the monthly cost of buying the vehicle from them based on the lowest interest rate they can offer. Do the same with the local dealership because they often have lower interest rate financing options.

By this method, you'll be able to make an informed decision. You'll know exactly what your monthly payment will be each month over the life of the loan.

Determine Trade-In Value

To determine what you should get for your car when you trade it in, use Kelley Blue Book (www.kbb.com). This is yet another website that's easy to navigate. Simply enter your car type, model, and age, and it gives a guideline for what your trade-in will be based on the condition. Have the dealership match or beat that price so you know you are being treated fairly.

By following these guidelines, you may not get the greatest deal in the world, but neither will you get ripped off. Everyone who buys a car thinks they got a great deal. Don't be one of those who realize later they got taken advantage of simply because they didn't have a plan, or they didn't do the appropriate research.

When to Buy

Few people think about the best time of year to make a car purchase, but it can make a difference. If you're not in a big hurry, and you have time to shop and compare, consider the time of year. The website www.TrueCar, notes that winter months are best for the deepest discounts. While those discounts may be available, it's also true that toward the end of the year inventories may be limited. That means January might be the best month.

Discounts are not as prevalent in spring because more people are out shopping, and oftentimes consumers are flush with their recent tax refund in the bank account. Dealers aren't as eager to offer discounts since they don't need to entice customers to buy–they're already eager shoppers.

Now that you have better insight as to making a car purchase, it's time to talk about where you will live. As a teen, you may be limited to your parents' home or a dorm room for a while. But those days will not last forever. Let's take a look.

CHAPTER 11

WHERE WILL YOU LIVE?

A ll Joey could talk about since he landed his job at the movie theater was his love of writing movie reviews. They were in Trav's bedroom, where Joey had his iPad up and was showing off his latest review on the blog he'd set up.

Travis wasn't about to let Joey know how impressed he was—but he *definitely was impressed*. Joey seemed to have hit on something he really loved doing. But he'd been talking on and on for quite some time and Trav was getting hungry and suggested they go down to the kitchen and hunt up some grub.

Halfway down the stairs, Trav, who was in the lead, stopped, put his hand up for Joey to stop, and put his finger to his lips. Joey froze.

Voices came from the kitchen and they picked up on the words, "Coach Palmer," and "wasn't it a shame," and "foreclosure," and "should have known better…"

The boys exchanged questioning looks. Trav shrugged, and

Joey shook his head. They listened a little longer, then Travis headed toward the kitchen. His parents looked surprised as the boys entered the room.

Joey spoke first. "So what're you all talking about? What about Coach Palmer? He's my favorite coach."

"What did you mean about foreclosure? What's that all about?" Trav asked, pulling out a bar stool and sitting at the counter.

Trav's parents looked at one another. His dad spoke first. "I'm sorry. We shouldn't have even mentioned it. We thought you two were sequestered in the outer regions."

"But Dave," Trav's mother said, "it's got to be common knowledge. It's not something you can hide."

"Common knowledge about what? Hide what?" Joey said, getting a bit agitated. "Hey, we're adults. We can handle this."

"Well, not quite," Travis's dad said, "but pretty darn close."

"So? Out with it. What about Coach Palmer."

Trav's mother waved them over to the table. "Let's sit down where we can talk." His mother was always the practical one.

"A few years ago," Dave told them, "Coach Palmer and his wife bought a house in the Oak Ridge addition. You know where that is, right?"

"Sure. Everybody knows that. Where the big fancy houses are," Joey said. "How could he do that on a coach's salary?"

Trav's mother answered the question. "His wife had a corporate position that seemed secure, and we've learned that she was the one who wanted to live in Oak Ridge."

"Well, if they had the means…" Trav started, but his father cut in.

"She was laid off."

"Wow." This from Joey. "So why didn't they just fold up and sell and get out?"

"Because they were upside down."

"Upside down?" Trav repeated. "What the heck does that mean?"

"It means they owed more on the house that it's currently worth."

"I didn't even know that was possible," said Travis. "How can that happen?"

"There are mortgages," his dad explained, "that allow interest-only payments for the first few years. This keeps payments low but doesn't pay anything toward the principal, and it doesn't build any equity."

"Soda, anyone?" Ella asked. All nodded and she headed to the fridge.

Dave continued. "This probably looked really inviting to Coach and his wife because it keeps payments low, but those payments didn't even cover the full interest costs. It's such a trap because after a few years, if the value of homes in the area goes down– which is exactly what happened to the Palmers—the home buyer now owes more than the original loan."

Ella came back with cold cans of soda and everyone grabbed one. "So once his wife lost her corporate job and corporate paycheck, they began to fall behind in payments. The domino effect begins. Not only can they not make payments, but they also cannot sell."

"Why can't they just sell it?" Joey asked. "I don't understand."

"Who would want to pay more for a house than it's worth?" David said. "And remember when a house sells, there are realtor fees and closing costs. This increases the amount of money that's owed as they try to leave the house. If they can't even afford the mortgage payments, how could they afford those added costs?"

"Wow." This from Joey.

"But the dominoes keep falling. Once you fall behind in payments, the foreclosure process begins. Next comes eviction."

"Eviction?" said Travis. "Isn't that when they come and *make* you get out? Man! That's awful."

"It is awful," his father agreed, "but so preventable. I would have to say wisdom wasn't at the heart of their purchase decision."

"Expect the best; prepare for the worst," Joey said.

Ella looked over at Joey. "That's a good one, Joey. Where'd you come up with that?"

"From a friend of ours," Travis answered for Joey.

"A friend of *his*," Joey corrected. "Her name is Sarah." Travis kicked him under the table.

Later, the boys were still talking about the mess Coach was in.

"I never realized before how important it is when you choose where you live and how you live," Trav said.

"We're so lucky," Joey said, "our folks would never do anything so dumb as pay too much for a house and get upside down."

Trav nodded. "Yeah. I heard Mom and Dad talking just the other day how they only had a few more years and we'd be mortgage-free."

"Your dad probably inherited his smarts from his father-in-law."

Travis laughed at that. "Could be. I think Grandpa Charlie had that kind of effect on everyone he met."

"I want to be like Grandpa Charlie," Joey said. Again.

· · · · · ● · · · · ·

The Choice of Where to Live

Travis and Joey learned a good lesson when they heard the account of what happened to their coach and his family. The phrase "living within your means" had taken on new meaning for them.

Choosing where to live boils down to whether you will rent or buy. Most teens, and even college students, are usually not to the financial point where they can buy a house; however, that event may come in the near future, so it's good to be informed ahead of time. In this chapter, we'll take a look at the pros and cons of these options.

Benefits of Renting

Flexibility

When you rent an apartment or house, it allows you to explore an area before making a long-term commitment to purchase a home. If you're uncertain about a specific neighborhood, renting allows time for research and discovery.

Career Uncertainty

In this day and time, job changes happen quite frequently. If there's any chance that you may face a change in the near future, it would be smarter to rent for a few years until your career becomes more stable. If you own a property, you might have second thoughts about that job change due to the hassle of selling before a move.

Income Uncertainty

Any change in your income could affect your ability to meet the demands of mortgage payments—such as in the case of the Palmer family. If uncertainty looms in the future, it's best to rent for a time.

Bad Credit

If you now have a history of bad credit, there's no better way to build that score back up than to create a pattern of on-time rental payments. This can help you build the type of credit rating needed to qualify for a mortgage.

No Maintenance Expenses.

One of the great benefits of renting is when the AC goes out (or other needed repairs), you don't call the heat and air repair guy; you call your landlord. They are responsible to fix everything that needs fixing.

Utilities (Sometimes) Included

In some instances, the landlord may pay for utilities such as water, sewer, garbage–perhaps even gas and electric. This is a great benefit to those who choose to rent.

Downside of Renting

One of the downsides of renting is that you have no control over rent increases. The property owner, whether it be an apartment or a single-family residence, makes the decision about rent increases.

Additionally, rent money is money that is not growing. Unlike mortgage payments, rent does not result in building equity.

Benefits of Ownership

Equity

When you rent a house, you are paying your landlord's mortgage or adding equity to his or her bank account. When you are paying down the mortgage on your own home, you increase your degree of ownership with every payment.

Nothing in real estate happens immediately. It takes about five to seven years for the costs of purchasing your home to be offset by the built-up equity–and possibly the increased value of the property.

Eventually, there will be enough equity to enable the owner to borrow against it. This should be used cautiously, but can be a big help if capital is needed, say, for starting a business.

Another benefit is that if interest rates drop, the owner can refinance for more favorable rates. This often leads to lower mortgage payments.

The family who plans well, can pay off their mortgage early. The family budget that has no mortgage payments means that money can be invested elsewhere and can grow into a sizeable nest egg.

Tax Deductions

Tax deductions are always a blessing, since so much of our money goes toward taxes (as we learned in Chapter 7). A homeowner is allowed to deduct mortgage interest and property taxes on their annual tax report.

If you meet certain requirements, the IRS won't apply a capital gains tax on profits from the sale of your home. You can keep the first $250,000 in profit you make when selling the home if you're single, or the first $500,000 if you're married.

Creative Control

When you are the owner, you get to decide how to paint, remodel, decorate, and so on. It's yours and you can do as you like. Need to move a wall and create another room? Go for it. That's a great benefit of being a home owner.

Maintenance Choices

If you own your own home, you decide how to approach maintenance–you can do it yourself or hire it done by a contractor. You can create the greenest lawn on the block, or cover the yard over with gravel and forget mowing. It's yours to do with as you like.

If there is a homeowner's association in your addition, you may be required to pay monthly fees and the association deals with some of the maintenance. Also there may be certain rules and restrictions regarding the appearance of your house and yard.

Perhaps you own a condominium. In that case, the dues pay for the maintenance and there are no lawns to mow or leaky roof to fix. But you still own your own space.

Is It Cheaper to Rent?

This can be a loaded question and can include a number of variables. It can depend on the market where you live. It can depend on whether you hate doing home improvement and maintenance projects–or love them.

You may want to use an aid such as *Zillow's Rent Vs Buy Calculator* to help determine if owning a home will be cheaper than renting over time. (http://www.zillow.com/rent-vs-buy-calculator/)

It's important to keep in mind that a house is an expensive investment—one that needs constant work and upkeep. There's no landlord to call to come right over and fix whatever has gone wrong.

Helpful Online Resources

When it comes time to shop for a house, you can do a great deal of shopping online. You can use sites such as www.realtor.com, and www.zillow.com. These sites allow you to enter in specific information such as the boundaries of a certain neighborhood, the price range, and size of house.

You can learn the history of the prices of houses that have recently been bought and sold. You can also learn how the price of a house you're interested in, compares to other homes in the area. This way you will know whether or not you're buying at market price. This is a great help when it comes time to negotiate the price. Having this kind of knowledge and information puts you ahead of the game. Always do you research. Buying a house is a major investment–it's not a purchasing decision where you want to make any major mistakes.

Top 10 mortgage tips for potential buyers:

11. Improve your creditworthiness

Your credit profile is important to a lender. While you're preparing to buy a home, be sure you're responsibly managing your current debt. Always pay your bills on time and chip away at your outstanding balances by paying more than the minimum. In most cases, lenders like to see a borrower with a debt-to-income ratio of 36% or less.

12. Save for a down payment

Although a 20% down payment on a mortgage is ideal, it's not mandatory. Many lenders expect buyers to put down at least 3%, aside from the Federal Housing Administration, which requires a 3.5% down payment. However, if you're interested in building sizable equity right away, stash a hefty amount of cash to take to the closing table. Additionally, do your due diligence to find out about any local down payment assistance programs.

13. Seek preapproval

Before you rush into house-hunting mode, get a mortgage preapproval. This process is used to help determine how much money you're qualified to borrow for a home purchase. Once you're preapproved, you'll have a more realistic expectation of which for-sale houses fall within your budget. You may qualify for a loan that is roughly 3 times your gross annual income.

14. Shop for a lender

The home buying process involves more than just chasing a favorable interest rate. You have to find the best mortgage lender for your financial situation. No two sets of lender fees are alike, so it's important to get loan estimates from multiple lenders before making a decision.

15. Research loan types

A fixed-rate mortgage isn't right for every homebuyer. Neither is an adjustable-rate mortgage. If you plan to stay put in a home to raise a family, you might consider a 30-year loan. Conversely, if you're moving in 10 years or less, an adjustable-rate mortgage, or ARM, could better suit you. Interest rates on ARMs are fixed for the first several years of the loan and often start out lower than rates on 30-year fixed loans. There are also jumbo loans, which are typically used to purchase luxury homes.

16. Consider your lifestyle

When you purchase a home, you're also investing in the community that surrounds it. More importantly, your home becomes central to every other aspect of your life. As you shop for homes, consider your work commute, nearby schools and any extracurricular activities in which you and your family might participate.

17. Remember to budget

Your monthly mortgage payment won't be the only expense you have as a homeowner. There's also homeowners' insurance, property taxes, maintenance costs and, more than likely, homeowners association fees, which is why it's necessary to stick to a budget. Use Bankrate.com's "How much house can I afford?" calculator to determine a feasible home loan amount.

18. Consult a professional

The home buying process is a challenging one, which is why it helps to have the assistance of qualified professionals. Ask questions of your lender and real estate agent, and reach out to a housing counseling agency approved by the U.S. Department of Housing and Urban Development for further guidance.

19. Don't forget the closing costs

Not only do you need a solid down payment for a home purchase, you'll have to pay closing costs. The loan estimate you receive after applying for a mortgage gives you an idea of the "cash to close," or the money you need to complete the transaction. There are some closing costs for which you can shop and save money, and others that are fixed.

20. Beef up your savings account

It's unwise to drain your savings to fund your down payment or closing costs and leave nothing in the account to cover emergencies. A useful rule of thumb is to stockpile 3 to 6 months' worth of living expenses. This deters you from tapping credit cards or loans and amassing more debt.

www.bankrate.com/finance/mortgages/mortgage-tips/

We've covered a lot of ground so far in this book. You've learned about credit, taxes, debt, making good and not-so-good buying decisions. But now let's talk about the more *magical* aspect of money and finances—how money grows.

CHAPTER 12

MONEY MAY NOT GROW ON TREES; BUT IT DOES GROW

Trav and Joey were walking to Grandma Bess's house. She said she wanted to see them, and neither had access to transportation that day. But since it was such a beautiful spring day, neither one minded the walk.

Out of the blue, Trav asked, "Do you know why Sarah's dad decided to become a financial counselor?"

"Well," Joey answered, "since you've been spending so much time at Sarah's house, I guess you know everything about the family. Pray tell—what *did* cause Mr. Carter to make his career choice?"

"Don't get smart—this is serious."

"Ah. Two weeks to graduation and already you're sounding more like Craig. Sheesh."

Trav gave his cousin a shoulder shove and sent him off the sidewalk. "Do you want to know or not?"

"I think I'm going to hear whether I want to know or not. Okay, give. I'm dying to know." He faked a stagger at these last words.

"Here's the deal. His parents were spend-spend-spend type of people. He said they had every type of credit card there was to be had. They took family cruises, and always had the best cars. But his parents never owned a house because they could never qualify for a mortgage."

"Sounds kinda like Coach Palmer. Living outside their means."

"Yeah, like that. Well, now that they're older, they have no resources and Mr. Carter has to take care of them. He told me that even as a teen, he knew there had to be a better way to manage money."

"So what did he do?"

"He studied and researched, and talked to people who had accumulated wealth. He learned what worked and what didn't work."

"Sounds like a really smart guy. He gonna be your father-in-law?"

Joey got another shove off the sidewalk. "I'm being serious, remember?"

"You being serious is so strange, I keep forgetting," Joey replied. "I can't get used to it. So what did he learn from these rich guys?"

"He said to me, 'Trav, money may not grow on trees, but it *can grow*.'"

"What did he mean by that?"

"He said this to me during one of those evenings when I was at their house, and when Sarah got a little impatient with her dad.

I guess she hears this stuff all the time, but I was fascinated. He started talking about compound interest, calculated investments, rate of growth, real estate investing, and all sorts of stuff."

"Sound a little boring to me."

"I was fascinated."

"You said that once."

Trav ignored him. "Just think about this, Joey. Money isn't just something to spend as quick as we get it. It's really a tool that can work *for* us."

"Trav, you're just so deep, I feel like I'm sinking." To change the subject, because he really was getting bored, Joey said, "Hey, I wonder what Grandma Bess wants to see us about?"

"I have no idea, but I think we're about to find out."

They found their grandma in her living room, dressed in her bright blue sweats as though she'd just come from the fitness center. After hugs and greetings, she had them sit down, and pointing to papers strewn about on the coffee table, she said. "I have something here that has to do with the two of you."

"That looks like important papers," Joey ventured.

"Important they are, my dear Joey," she replied. "You'll remember that I told you that your Grandpa Charlie and I sure weren't thinking about grandchildren when we were a young married couple. But that doesn't mean we weren't thinking about all of you later!

"When you were first born, your grandpa and I created a trust fund to help with your college expenses. This is part of the reason why Charlie was always looking for ways to make his money grow.

And I have to admit," she added with a chuckle, "he did a darn good job of it."

"Wow." This from Joey.

"But," Trav said, "it never seemed like you two had a lot of money. I mean, not enough to set up a trust fund for all four of your grandchildren."

"All things are relative, Travis."

"Meaning?"

"Such as what is meant by 'a lot of money.' If you mean we didn't live in the fanciest house or drive the latest car, you're right. Here's the important thing, boys—it's never a matter of how much money you have, it's all about *what you do with the money you have.*"

Trav turned to Joey. "Sarah's father says that, too."

"Well, he's absolutely right. You don't need a whole boatload of money to invest and make it grow. You can start small and just let it grow."

"How did grandpa make money grow?" Trav wanted to know.

"A few solid stocks here and there, mutual funds, his rent properties. Nothing speculative, just wise investing. And then giving it time to grow. Having patience."

"So what's a trust fund, anyway?" Joey asked.

"It's money that's in your name, it belongs to you, but—since your grandpa was no fool—there are stipulations to your receiving it."

"You mean there's strings attached."

"I guess you could look at it that way," Grandma Bess said smiling. "But Charlie meant for this money to go toward your education, and part of the stipulation is that it be applied toward tuition, and that you make good grades. It's nothing that two smart boys like you can't handle." She handed each one of them an envelope. "The particulars are in here."

Then she added, "I'm not saying there's enough here to pay your total tuition. But it'll take both of you on down the road toward a debt-free education. Thanks to Charlie."

"And you," said Travis, coming over to give his grandma a hug.

"I want to be like Grandpa Charlie," Joey said. Again. And he, too, gave his grandma a big hug.

· · · · · ● · · · ·

Differences in How People Handle Money

Travis and Joey were beginning to see how differently people viewed money and how they managed money. Their coach and his wife who made foolish decisions and lost their house; Mr. Carter's parents whom he witnessed spending recklessly with no thought of the future; Mr. Carter himself, who then not only wanted to learn about finances, but wanted a career that involved helping others manage their money. They saw how their own parents were prudent with money, and were careful not to overextend. Then, of course, their much-loved grandparents, who had enough foresight to actually put money away for their grandchildren. This alone had a huge impact on the boys.

In this chapter, we want to take a look at how money can grow. This is in no way an in-depth discussion, but simply an overview. Hopefully, you'll want to know more and will do your own research (or treasure hunt) on your own.

Compound Interest

What is meant by compound interest? It was Albert Einstein who called compounding "the greatest mathematical discovery of all time." It works like this. You put an amount of money into an investment that earns interest. When the interest is earned and the original amount grows, nothing is withdrawn–nothing is taken out. (This is not the money you *spend*.)

Now another interest period comes around and at this point you not only earn interest on the original amount, you also earn interest on the accumulated interest. At first it appears very small and inconsequential, but it's rather like a snowball that has been sent careening downhill, it picks up speed, and more and more snow, as it rolls along.

That's the basic theory, but let's look at compound interest in action. Let's say you made the decision to put away $100 every year. Stay with me here, because this is just an example to show how powerful compound interest can be. You're putting away $100 each year and let's say your rate of interest is 11% (which is not an unreasonable amount–but that's another subject).

On the following page is a table that shows at various periods of time exactly how much money you will accumulate. Are you a little surprised at the final total?

Year	Amount
5	$639
10	1,700
15	3,488
20	6,500
25	11,576
30	20,129
35	34,541
40	58,827

Be Consistent and Patient

This may seem almost unbelievable, but it's true. This is not money you had to work for, this is money that is *working for you*. It's money that is *growing*, just like Mr. Carter and Grandpa Charlie talked about.

What's your part? To be consistent and patient. And disciplined enough to leave this "seed money" alone. Not to dip into it just because some new gadget is now on sale at the best price ever.

If this chart blows your mind, let's take it a step further. What if you put away $200 a year instead of $100? The growth potential is amazing.

Compounding depends on three factors:

- How much money you invest
- How much time it spends growing
- Its rate of growth

The beauty of this kind of money growth is that it doesn't

require that you go without. It's much like Grandpa Charlie did, simply putting money away on a regular basis, for a specific purpose. You don't have to watch over it day after day; it's doing its own thing without your help.

Information on Investing

Walk into any bookstores or library, go to the section on investing, and you will find a wide array of books on the shelves. There's no lack of information on this subject. For our discussion, I want to give an overview of just a few investment opportunities to get ideas flowing.

If you think you are too young to begin investing, think again. If you think you have to be wealthy to invest, you have another *think again* coming. You can start small; and you can start young. That's good news for you, and hopefully you'll warm up to the idea of using some of your money for investments that will grow over the years.

Let's review a few possibilities.

Savings Account

If you've already set up a checking account, as was discussed in Chapter 5, it's a good idea to set up a savings account at the same time in the same bank. While savings accounts earn only a small amount of interest, still they can be an important aspect in your money management plan.

Once you have a *receptacle* for your money (your savings account), you are much more likely to get in the habit of savings. Make it a habit to put a certain amount in your savings account with each and every paycheck you receive. You are learning to "pay yourself first," and you're not as likely to make a foolish purchase that you will regret later.

CDs – Certificate of Deposit

A certificate of deposit (CD) is a savings certificate entitling the bearer to receive interest. A CD bears a maturity date, a specified fixed interest rate and can be issued in any denomination. CDs are generally issued by commercial banks and are insured by the FDIC. The term of a CD generally ranges from one month to five years.

www.investopedia.com/terms/c/certificateofdeposit.asp

If you are looking for a place to stash your savings, but want a little more than what a bank savings account earns, you might consider purchasing CDs. When your money is in a CD, you will not be as tempted to spend it because you will incur a penalty to make the withdrawal. Check with your bank to see what's available.

Let's say that you purchase a $10,000 CD with an interest rate of 5% compounded annually and a term of one year. At year's end, the CD will have grown to $10,500. This means you have an extra $500 that you did not have to work for. (Again, we're talking about how money grows.)

As a teen, you may not have ten grand to tuck away (if you did, you'd probably buy a car, right?). But this example gives you an idea of exactly how CDs help you to save, and to earn interest.

Stocks

The Definition of a Stock. Plain and simple, stock is a share in the ownership of a company. Stock represents a claim on the company's assets and earnings. As you acquire more stock, your ownership stake in the company becomes greater. Whether you say shares, equity, or stock, it all means the same thing.

www.investopedia.com/university/stocks/stocks1.asp

You may have heard that trading in the stock market is risky and dangerous. And that's true, it can be. On the other hand, there are stable, strong businesses that have been around for years, and will be around for years in the future. Purchasing shares in such businesses is not at all speculative. Shares that are held over years not only earn interest, but some earn *dividends.* If you reinvest that extra income, this means your money grows at a greater exponential rate.

You will need your parents to co-sign before you can enter into trades (and you'll probably want their input, anyway).

A dividend is a distribution of a portion of a company's earnings, decided by the board of directors, to a class of its shareholders. Dividends can be issued as cash payments, as shares of stock, or other property.

www.investopedia.com/terms/d/dividend.asp

Bonds

Bonds, in general, are considered a safer investment than

stocks, since you know the amount of fixed income (interest) you will receive from the bonds, and for how long. This does not mean that there is no risk with bonds, but the risk varies with the type of bond you purchase. From the outset, you have some idea of how much risk you are assuming.

Most bonds require a minimum investment—it can be $1,000 or $5,000. During difficult and uncertain economic times when the stock market might be depressed, investors tend to move their money into bonds. Bonds are also a good way to diversify your portfolio. Most investors have at least part of their money invested in bonds. And although you do not hear about it as often, the bond market is actually larger than the stock market.

Mutual Funds

A mutual fund is an investment vehicle that is made up of a pool of funds collected from many investors for the purpose of investing in securities such as stocks, bonds, money market instruments and similar assets. Mutual funds are operated by money managers, who invest the fund's capital and attempt to produce capital gains and income for the fund's investors. A mutual fund's portfolio is structured and maintained to match the investment objectives stated in its prospectus.

www.investopedia.com/terms/m/mutualfund.asp

A person who invests in mutual funds has their investment spread over a wide number of stocks and securities, and because of this, the risk is much lower than purchasing individual stock shares. Investors who look for low volatility and low risk, often turn to mutual funds.

REIT – Real Estate Investment Trust

> *A REIT is a type of security that invests in real estate through property or mortgages and often trades on major exchanges like a stock. REITs provide investors with an extremely liquid stake in real estate. They receive special tax considerations and typically offer high dividend yields.*
>
> www.investopedia.com/terms/r/reit.asp

REITs can be thought of as a type of mutual fund in the real estate industry. Again, the risk is spread over a wide variety of types of real estate–this ranges from hospitals to hotels to shopping centers. REITs are an interesting segment of the investing arena.

Summing Up

How you look at money–or how you perceive money–will affect many areas of your life. Hopefully, this chapter helped you to see that money is more than something that comes into your hands and allows you to buy a new pair of Nikes or the latest gadget that technology has to offer. Money has the power to fund your future; it has the power to create a lifestyle for you that is secure and comfortable.

You have the power to unleash that money-magic by seeking for ways to grow money rather than simply spend money. And the younger you begin to grow money, the greater the growth.

It's all pretty exciting when you think about it.And as we learn in the Epilogue, it's *your future!*

EPILOGUE

INVEST IN YOUR FUTURE BECAUSE NO ONE ELSE WILL

The high school library was a flurry of green and gold bedlam as hundreds of graduating seniors were getting into their caps and gowns. Parents, class sponsors, teachers, and other sundry adults scurried about assisting and lending to the general chaos in the place.

Spotting Joey in another part of the room, Trav called him over. Joey moved his direction, maneuvering through the press. "Yeah, Cuz. Whatcha need?"

"Hey, you dork. That's *not* how you wear a mortarboard."

Joey had his cap mashed on the back of his head with the tassel hanging straight down.

"My motor what? What're you talking about, Trav?"

Trav reached out and pulled the cap off Joey's head. "This," he said, "is a mortarboard. And the square lays flat." He pointed to his own on his head. "Like this."

"Well, other guys—and a few gals too—wear it like this."

"We, my good buddy, are not *other guys.* And definitely are not *other gals.* Now put it on right. That way when it's time to move the tassel, you won't be reaching halfway down your back."

"Travis, Travis. Such a stickler for details," Joey said shaking his head. "The big moment we've been waiting for, and you fuss about my motorboat."

"Mortarboard."

"Motor, mortar… Whatever. And hey, talk about looking good." He reached out and touched the National Honor Society stole hanging around Travis's neck. "This looks great on you." He leaned over and said in a stage whisper. "All due to late study nights with Sarah? Eh?"

Trav returned with a fake punch on his cousin's arm. "Watch it there. You're gonna get hurt."

Just then they heard the call to line up for their grand entrance into the auditorium.

During the ceremony, Joey was recognized for the movie review blog he'd developed that had captured national attention. Travis was pretty proud of his dorky cousin.

Both Travis and Joey were already enrolled in their local community college. Joey was signed up for classes in business and marketing. He found he was fascinated with all facets of online marketing. He'd been spending time with the young entrepreneur, Terrance, hoping to step into the position of a student intern. The possibility was looking good.

Travis planned to spend two years at community college, then advance to state university to finish up—hopefully with a degree in bioengineering. He and his parents were already scouring about for any and all types of scholarships and grants to help with his expenses. This along with the trust fund from Grandpa Charlie, meant they were well on their way to paring down college expenses to a bare minimum.

Because both of the cousins were planning to stay in their community–at least for a couple of years–they were both able to retain their part-time jobs.

Presently, they were locked in a friendly competition to see who could build the biggest savings account the fastest.

. . . . . ● . . . . .

The Years Ahead

Whether you're in high school, about to graduate, or are a recent graduate, stop and reflect for a moment. Think back to seventh grade. Now think how quickly those few years sped by. If you're a senior now, that was five years ago.

Guess what? The next five years are going to fly by just as fast, or faster. Before you know it, you'll be a young adult in your twenties. What will life be like for you then?

Every person is different; every person has different dreams and aspirations. Looking at the future can be somewhat confusing, and at times even overwhelming, but you can begin now to create financial goals for your twenties. Here are a few ideas for you to consider.

Learn All You Can About Finances and Money Management

Have you ever thought about how odd it is that even though money plays a huge part in our everyday lives, we are taught very little about money and money management? Even in families, there seems to be more emphasis on discussions about dating and drugs than in investing and money growth. This is sad, because knowledge is power. The more you know, the better money manager you will become

Create a Budget

The subject of budgeting was covered in Chapter 6. Keeping track of your money and where it goes is crucial when it comes to money management. Once you are on your own, with your own bills to pay, everything will all of a sudden look very different. It's the end of the month, the rent is due, and you are out of money. Whoa! What happened? Lack of planning; lack of budgeting.

A budget will help you to see exactly where you can cut back and be able to make ends meet. It will also help you to see how much you can put away each payday to "pay yourself first."

The Need for Health Insurance

The subject of health insurance has been touched on earlier, but because it's so crucial, it bears repeating.

This may a difficult expenditure for you as a young adult. Because you're young and healthy, it seems like an unnecessary expense, but one hospital stay could be financially devastating.

Shop. Investigate. Ask questions. Find out what's available for you. If you have a job find out what might be offered through your work. If you don't have a job that offers health insurance, search your state's insurance exchange for an affordable plan.

If you're healthy, opt for a high deductible plan. Also you can open a health savings account (HSA). You'll pay a lower monthly premium, and the money you set aside in your HSA is tax-deductible.

Always Have an Emergency Fund.

There will always be emergencies that pop up from time to time, such as car repair, for example. Instead of pulling out the plastic and paying interest, have an emergency fund set aside. Why pay extra if you don't have to?

When you have an emergency fund stashed away, you will never feel strapped for cash, even if you're not earning a lot of money. In fact, it gives you a sense of comfort knowing that money is there.

Get Rid of Credit Card Debt

No matter where you are in life, if you got off on the wrong foot when you first started using credit cards, make it your highest priority to pay these off any balances. Credit cards are a huge drain on your money. You're paying money for no return—and instead, that money could be growing like I talked about in Chapter 12.

Look at it like this—if you pay off a credit card bill that is charging you 14% interest, in essence, you're paying yourself 14% guaranteed, and tax free. What a great return on investment!

Once they are all paid off, consider getting rid of them altogether. Of course, there are arguments for keeping a credit card, such as for emergencies, earning rewards, and so on. And it's true that when used properly, a credit card can be a useful tool.

The trouble is it's laden with so many possible pitfalls (accidentally missing a payment, added fees, rate hikes, etc.), that the downside often outweighs the benefits.

Hide those credit cards, forget about them, and test yourself for six months. See that it *is* possible to navigate life without a credit card. Try paying cash for everything with your debit card, or actual cash. You will never regret this decision.

Track Your Credit Score Early On

You may not be in the market to purchase a home while in your twenties, still you will need good credit for other purchases, such as a car.

It's a good idea to start tracking how the banks view your creditworthiness by requesting a free yearly credit report and checking your number every year or so.

As was mentioned earlier, this habit also helps catch any illegal loans that might have been taken out in your name by identity thieves. The earlier you catch fraudulent loans, the easier it is to do something about it.

Your Retirement Account

Suppose you set aside $1,000 a year from age 25 to age 64 in a retirement account that earns 5% a year (historically, stocks return about 8%, but we'll be conservative). That's $39,000 total you invest. By the time you turn 65, you'll have $126,840. If you don't get started with saving until you're 35, you'll only have $69,760. Starting just ten years earlier would have doubled your total. Yes, doubled.

Get a Financial Life: Personal Finance In Your Twenties and Thirties

by Beth Kobliner

We've talked about two steps so far—starting your emergency fund and paying off those high-interest credit cards. The next step will be to start a retirement account.

If you have a job that offers a 401k plan, sign up. If you don't know which investments fund your account, go with index funds. If your employer offers 401k matching, contribute at least the minimum amount for which you're eligible to receive the matching funds. But the more you can invest, the better.

It's a sad state of affairs that so many young employees pass up all this free money (matching funds) because they feel they can't afford to pay money into a 401k plan. It's a failure to take a serious look into the future.

If your job doesn't offer a 401k or if you're self-employed, you can open a Roth IRA account. Your bank likely offers one or you can use an online broker service like Vanguard or Fidelity. Fund it with index funds.

Make it your goal to contribute at the very least, 5% of your gross income into your retirement account.

Set up a system to pay down debt, increase your emergency fund, and then ratchet up your savings rate. This is a great 3-step plan to financial security.

Multiple Streams of Income

Saving money when you are in your twenties is a good thing, but it's also a good thing to find other ways to bring in extra income.

Get in the habit of creating multiple streams of income. This habit not only helps to build your personal wealth, but it will serve you well as you get older.

Even the most secure-feeling job will not always be secure. You can't always rely on that steady income from your 9-to-5 job. (Remember the account of Coach Palmer and his wife.) Don't put all your eggs in one basket—always be looking for other sources of cash coming in.

What type of micro-businesses can you run when you're not doing your day job? It could be something as simple as mowing lawns on the weekends or writing resumes. Get creative. If you've got a skill, there will always be someone willing to pay you for it.

Set Long-Term Financial Goals

The decade of your twenties is a great time to get even more serious about your future and the financial goals that you want to achieve. You're past those flighty teen years; you're seeing life from a different perspective.

Whatever those goals are, write them down and begin to take the steps to make them happen.

Closing Thoughts

It is hard to make money, but it is very easy to spend it. Corporations and retailers in America are experts in creating consumers (also known as *victims*) for their brands.

Focus on what you need rather than what you want. When you buy a cell phone or purchase direct TV for entertainment, choose your packages to meet your basic needs, not to make those companies wealthier.

When you buy clothes or shoes, shop at retail outlets (Nordstrom Rack, Ross, TJ Max) to avoid spending more than money than necessary.

Going out to eat should be a treat and not a lifestyle. Learn to cook (it's not difficult—really). You can learn on YouTube! Create a budget and shop at stores such as Costco and Sam's Club. You can buy food items in bulk, freeze, and ultimately reduce costs.

Don't waste money on $5 coffees. Again, let the expensive coffee be an occasional treat rather than a daily habit.

Pack your lunches for work instead of spending $10-$15 every day. Put pencil to paper to prove to yourself how fast those bought-lunches add up. Calculate exactly how much it costs per month. Then per year. It will make those packed lunches much more appealing.

When you're traveling, look for deals on flights, cruises, and hotels on websites such as Expedia.com, Hotel.com, Priceline.com and Orbitz.com. Compare prices on each website for the best deals.

Rent movies on Netflix.com. Like eating out, let movies at the theater be a special night and not the norm. Why pay $10 to $20 a ticket, plus sodas and popcorn for another $5 to $10? Opt to download movies at home for a bargain price and pop your own popcorn.

It all comes down to being true to yourself. Do a check on yourself–do you make buying decisions to impress others? Or because they are wise buying decisions?

There's a much better way to be impressive. And that is having money saved and invested for your future, having money to make choices without getting into debt, and having financial security for an unexpected event. Now *that's* impressive!

By reading this book and putting into action what you've learned here, you will be well on your way to having that financial security.

I wish you all the best!

APPENDIX

Below are the requirements and restrictions for attaining a driver's license in the state of Florida. As you can see, it's a structured set of laws. I've used my home state of Florida as an example, but you will want to check with your own state to know the requirements that you must meet.

Graduated Driver Licensing Law

In an effort to minimize risks associated with first-time drivers, the Florida Department of Highway Safety and Motor Vehicles (DHSMV) has implemented a graduated driver licensing (GDL) law.

If you're under 18 years old, you must complete the following stages of the Florida GDL program:

- Learner's permit (15 years old)

- Intermediate driver's license/provisional license (16 to 17 years old).

- Full privilege driver's license (18 years old).

In order to apply for a Florida learner's permit, you must be at least 15 years old and have completed the Florida **Traffic Law and Substance Abuse Education (TLSAE)** course.

You must visit your local FL DMV office with (checklist):

- A completed Parental Consent for a Driver Application of a Minor (Form HSMV 71142).

- Proof of your **identity** (e.g. certified U.S. birth certificate).

- Proof of your **Social Security number** (e.g. Social Security card).

- Proof that you have completed a TLSAE course

- Proof of your Florida **residential address**.

Once you provide the required documents mentioned above, you'll need to pass a vision exam, hearing test, and the DMV written test.

With your Florida learner's permit in your possession, you can only drive during daytime hours for the first 3 months. After this time, you will be allowed to drive until 10 p.m.

You must always be with a licensed driver who is at least 21 years old and is sitting in the front passenger seat.

Before moving on to your provisional license:

- You must practice driving for at least 50 hours.

- 10 hours of the total 50 hours must be driven at night.

To move on to your intermediate driver's license (provisional license), you must:

- Be at least 16 years old.

- Have had your Florida learner's permit for at least 1 year without incident.

- Have completed a minimum of 50 hours of behind-the-wheel driving experience (10 hours must be at night).

You must visit the Florida DHSMV and:

- Submit your FL learner's license

- Pass a driving test OR present a DMV road test waiver from your Driver's Ed course.

- Submit certification that you've completed the required behind-the-wheel hours.

Depending on your age, you'll need to follow certain driving restrictions while on your intermediate driver's license.

- 16 years old: You may drive unsupervised, but only between 6 a.m. and 11 p.m.

- 17 years old: You may only drive unsupervised between 5 a.m. and 1 a.m.

Regardless of your age, you can drive at any time of day if:

- You're supervised by a licensed driver who is at least 21 years old. OR

- You're driving to and from work.

Once you turn 18 years old, your provisional driver's license will turn into a full-privilege driver's license. You will no longer need to follow any driving restrictions or have a licensed driver supervising you.

www.ingramcontent.com/pod-product-compliance
Lightning Source LLC
Chambersburg PA
CBHW050506210326
41521CB00011B/2346